Denys Parsons was educated at Eton and the universities of Munich and London. He has been a research chemist, educational and industrial film-maker and a group manager at the National Research Development Corporation. From 1973 he was head of press and public relations at the British Library. He now combines a flourishing piano tuning business with writing, and translating and editing for technical translation bureaux.

He started collecting funny misprints as a schoolboy and his first book of them was published by Macdonald in 1952 after rejection by 12 other publishers; five more followed. His major work was the *Directory of Tunes*, published in 1975, and he also compiled an offbeat shopping guide *What's Where in London* which went into seven editions. Denys Parsons is married with two sons and lives in north London.

D1603833

Also available from FUTURA

TOO FUNNY FOR WORDS

Much Too Funny For Words

DENYS PARSONS

drawings by Anton

Futura

A Futura Book

First published in Great Britain in 1986
by Futura Publications, a Division of
Macdonald & Co (Publishers) Ltd
London & Sydney

ISBN 0 7088 3085 4

Typeset in Baskerville by Fleet Graphics, Enfield, Middlesex

Printed in Great Britain by
William Collins, Glasgow

Futura Publications
Macdonald & Co (Publishers) Ltd
Greater London House
Hampstead Road
London NW1 7QX

A BPCC plc Company

INTRODUCTION

Here is another collection of hilarious misprints, solecisms, and other tomfoolery culled from newspapers and magazines. As far back as 1950 I began to suspect that such errors were inspired by a mischievous character who was in the habit of lurking in newspaper offices, causing these momentary aberrations of journalists. I named that scoundrel Gobfrey Shrdlu, and derived his name from a set of keys on the compositor's type-setting machine – SHRDLU corresponds to QWERTY on the typewriter.

I am sometimes asked whether I have invented any of the items in my collection. The answer is an emphatic NO. I would have thought that the genuineness of most of the items was self-evident. Who, for example, could have thought of inventing these two: 'Five thugs last night pulled the British passenger ship *Capetown* clear of a sandbank', and 'LONELY LADY, 43, with little dog, seeks post.'

For me laughter is almost the sole object of life. If you know of funnier books than *Too Funny for Words* and *Much Too Funny for Words*, I shall be most grateful for their titles. Now turn these pages and experience that pardoxically pleasant sensation as your sides begin to split with laughter.

The Judge said: 'You deceived this girl in exactly the same way as you have tried to deceive me. You attracted her into marriage and left her in the lurch with two children.'

Plymouth Weekly Gazette

NEW MAGISTRATE WELCOMED AT HAY

DRUNK IN CHARGE OF A BICYCLE

Brecon and Radnor Express

Without a word of warning the cows dashed out.

Motor Cycling

Riding at speed on their bicycles, dogs frequently chase the boys – and in some cases the owners think it is amusing.

Rhodesian Paper

Thanksgiving Day, Thursday, November 24th, will be observed with the Service of Morning Prayer at 9 o'clock. The choir will sing appropriate music. There will not be a sermon, Let us Thank God for Our Blessings!

St. Andrew's Church,
Harrisburg, PA.

The Vicar, the Rev. C.O. Marston, reported an increased number of communicants during the year. He also stated that the death watch beetle had been confirmed in the Church.

Banbury Guardian

Motor vehicle safety belts must be installed rigidly enough to withstand a sudden thirst.

Trenton Times

Although there are estimated to be over 50,000 different kinds of living insects, only 60 species are definitely known to be disease carriers. Enormous quantities of these are exported by New Zealand, during one season she sent to Britain 85,000 tons.

Malay Paper

Two tablespoonfuls of paraffin oil added to the foot-path will relieve and refresh aching feet.

Local Paper

A specially qualified public health inspector has been sent to Orleansville to detect the presence of rats and eventually to work out a programme of extermination.

395 applications for adoption have been sent in to the authorities concerned and numerous offers of hospitality are being considered by the public health service.

Algerian Paper

HAMPSTEAD BOROUGH ELECTION. This qualification entitles you to the Local Government Vote at 21, and the wife of any local Government elector at 30.

Electioneering Pamphlet

They took with them an Irish terrier dog and a brown sheep dog – both pets. Both were wearing horn-rimmed glasses.

Manchester Paper

She cried out in agony. And at that instant she heard a horse whisper behind her.

Indian Paper

Mrs. B – topped her grey lace bodice with a black chiffon skirt.

Washington Post

Within these fashion brackets are the new evening and dinner dresses that reach from just above the ankle to mid-calf.

The World-Telegram

To William and Kay Stout Martin, a son, Arthur Richard, Jr., on February 21.

To William and Kay Stout Martin, a son, William Garrett, on March 16.

Wilson Alumnae Quarterly

The police are trying to trace the relatives of a four months old baby found on a doorstep. It was dressed in clothing of very poor quality, and had been much laundered.

Surrey Paper

Mrs. Collins says she is not bothered that the baby did not turn out to be a girl, as she half expected.

New Zealand Weekly.

Mr. Thorbury was born in Victoria and immediately entered the engineering profession.

Vancouver Paper

AUDIENCE TRIED TO SPOIL PLAY
BUT ST. CHAD'S PLAYERS SUCCEEDED

Sunderland Echo

The marriage of Miss Anna Bloch and Mr. Willis Dashwood, which was announced in this paper a few weeks ago, was a mistake and we wish to correct.

Colorado Paper

WEDDING. At St. Mary's Church. Captain B—— to Violent Vera, daughter of Mr. and Mrs. J.B.L——.

Calcutta Paper

Mrs. Smithson – cheque and magnifying glass.

A huge collar of white fox fur successfully concealed the greater part of Mrs. David T——'s face.

Mr. and Mrs. Raymond Tibbetts, 627 Main Street, are the parents of a son named Teddy Roy, born Sunday at Dukes Hospital to Mr. and Mrs. Charles Hilleman of 526 East Canal Street.

Another performance of the pantomime is to be given in the Parish Hall, and this will give all those who missed seeing it another chance of doing so.

Miss Ruby Yates suddenly reveals a delicious sense of comedy, and is quite irresistible in black pyjamas, over her kidneys and bacon.

For some weeks now this method has been tried out at the Guildhall by members of the County Council staff. It is now considered foolproof.

Alderman S—— said the Council ought to be given the whole truth that there was still sufficient coal in the city to last five weeks if nobody used it.

Mr. John M'Fadden was re-appointed to wind, oil, and keep the Town Clerk in order.

Vocalists who sang the quartet very beautifully were Miss Jackman, Miss Mountford, Mrs. Jackman, and Mr. Palmer; the latter's rendering of 'Honk, Honk, the Lark' was full of charm.

Belfast Paper

We regret that our medical contributor is ill and therefore not able to write his weekly column 'How to be Healthy' at present.

North Country Paper

PROGRAMME

3.0	Hymns of Praise. Films.
3.45	'HUNGRY MEN'
4.15	Question Time.
4.30	Tea and buns.
6.0	'I was HUNGRY – SICK'.
6.45	'WHAT DO WE DO?' Open Forum.
7.45	Prayers.

London Missionary Society Programme

Its daily tasks are freed for ever from mechanism and insignificance for every man who knows that his fidelity in doing them makes him a fellow-worker (by arrangement with *The Times*) with God.

Rhodesian Paper

The new decree increases the French Customs Duties by thirty per cent, except for newsprint and cellulose used in the manufacture of sausages and certain cheese.

Chinese Paper

Just to let you know that your patient has been booked for her confinement under Miss Watson's car, on the recommendation of the Public Health Authority,

Letter received by Doctor

Come to the GOSPEL HALL,

67 Victoria Street, tomorrow night at 8.30
and hear of
'HELL – Where it is; and what it's like.'

Lighting, seating, heating, and shelter provided for all who wish to come inside. No collection.

Announcement in Belfast Telegraph

BISCUITS TO BE CHEAPER

GOOD PROFITS FROM RUBBER SOLES

North Country Paper

American Electric Blanket for sale, new. Owner leaving. Rosepink colour.

Advert. in Sunday Paper

Gobfrey Shrdlu clearly intends that when reading certain items we should sit back and try to visualise the scene. The following seven items seem to me particularly apt for visual appreciation.

Our picture shows Mr. Robert Tenter rolling the lawn with his fiancée, Miss Elizabeth Briarcliffe.

Bucks Paper

The Churchillian jaw was outthrust and the Prime Minister thumped the despatch box with a heavy fish.

Canadian Paper

So they set off. The Chief Constable with his brown cane tucked under his right arm. Chief Superintendent C.F. Broughton next – carrying nothing. Detective-Inspector E.G. Westland wore just a gas mask.

North London Paper

It was from an aerial slung between these masts that Melba, in 1920, sang the first broadcast music.

Evening Paper

'Mr. Perkins might be able to help you,' she said, as she took down a dusty lodger from the shelf.

Weekly Magazine

WANTED, Cigarette Makers (female) round and flat.

Advert. in Daily Chronicle

Slough Borough babies have their big chance at the baby show. Entries can be made on the ground and during the evening the last eight will contest the Berks and Bucks darts championship.

Windsor, Slough & Eton Express

Our motto is to give our customers the lowest prices and workmanship.

Sign at Dry Cleaners

Dear Madam,
With reference to your blue raincoat, our manufacturers have given the garment in question a thorough testing, and find that it is absolutely waterproof. If you will wear it on a dry day, and then take it off and examine it you will see that our statement is correct.
Your obedient servants,
Blank & Co., Drapers.

The cause of the explosion is unknown, but it is assumed that some combustible matter was among the coal.

Dorset Paper

ADDRESS (10 minutes) . . . Rev. J.B.C——
ANTHEM . . . 'It is enough' – Handel.

Church Notice Board

We are most grateful to those who so kindly repaired the dilapidated hassocks for the Church. Let us kneel on them.

Wiltshire Church Paper

Miss Yolande Lessard, sister of the bride, was maid of honor and wore a white ninon skirt, matching ostrich plumes in her hair and carried a royal blue brother of the bride, and Marcel. The bridegroom was attended by his velvet muff covered with pink roses.

Portland Press Herald

Students who marry during their course will not be permitted to remain in college. Further, students who are already married must either live with their husbands or make other arrangements with the dean.

Syllabus of an Ohio College

The First Aid treatment for a broken rib is to apply a tight bandage after you have made the patient expire.

Manchester Paper

The Crewe committee has arranged to apply the vaccine to 20 calves in October and three months later five or six more will be inoculated. Later some of both lots will be killed for the post-mortem examination, and if it is likely to prove beneficial, human beings will be similarly treated.

Australian Paper

Members will look forward to a River Trip this year as a change from a Trip to the River.

From a Club Journal

YOUNG PEOPLE'S SOCIETY. Everyone is invited. Tea and Social Hour at 6.15. Mrs. Smith will sin.

St. Louis Church Programme

A well-rounded ladies programme is now in process. of being worked up.

Journal of the Electro-chemical Society

Mrs. Charles, one of the cyclists, suffered from bruises to both legs, and her husband, Mr. Charles.

Dorset Paper

A committee of ladies, with Mrs. Roberts as leader, threw themselves into the tea, which proved a master-piece.

Devon Paper

Out of over 40 entries the following emerged as winners: Pet with the most amusing appearance . . . Mrs. C. Smith.

Birmingham Paper

All members will participate in the annual club luncheon. Owing to the large numbers it is deemed desirable to eat on the first day those whose surnames commence with any letters from A to M.

South African Paper

The party went by way of Ockendon, Bulphan, and Laindon, and the sea was reached about 1 o'clock. The tide was out, a thoughtful arrangement by the secretary.

Local Paper

The Mayor then raised the punch bowl to his lips, remarking: 'And now prosperity to all the people of B——, and prospezity to uor godo old tiwn.' (Applause.)

Report of Local Function

A Grand Jury in Los Angeles have indicted welter-weight boxer Art Aragon on a charge of offering a bride to an opponent.

Bradford Telegraph & Argus

Four riders cleared the course of about 800 yards with 14 obstacles, including Miss Richardson (Britain) on Cobler.

Scottish Sunday Express

WHY KILL THE WIFE?
LET US DO YOUR DIRTY WORK

Laundry Leaflet

FOR SALE – an absolutely perfect gentleman's bicycle.

Irish Paper

He was a Fellow of the Institute of Chemists, and a Fellow of the Chemises Society.

Irish Paper

Convection currents in the underlying rocks provide the energy and mechanical requirements needed to make possible the gradual drift or motion of woman's pale green two-piece suit on April 17th.

West Country Paper

At about one o'clock when the eclipse was on the sun, I saw a most beautiful star shining very bright, and I pointed this out to three ladies who were watching the eclipse in a bath of water. Is this an unusual occurrence?

Letter in West London Paper

LOW CONVERSATION ALLOWED
Notice in Public Gallery

Applications from bona-fide journalists, whether newspaper men* or press photographers, will be welcome.

*Under the rules, man embraces woman.
Advert. in Trade Paper

19

WANTED – Man to take care of cow that does not smoke or drink.

Advert. in South Carolina Paper

Gardeners should waste no time. Tie your pants in now before the south-easters blow.

Advert. in Cape Paper

BLOTTING PAPER WILL NOT
BE PROVIDED UNTIL
THE PUBLIC STOPS TAKING IT AWAY

Notice in Village Post Office

Mr. Sturgess said he would take up his duties as soon as the Council could find him a house. The commitee decided, on the recommendation of the surveyor, to place a manhole at the corner of Chase Road.

Local Paper

Thank God we have a Prime Minister who does not always wait to cross a bridge until he comes to it.

Letter in The Times

I am sending you my marage certificate and six children there were seven but one died You only sent six back her name was fanny and was baptised on a half sheet of paper by the reverend Thomas.

Letter received by Army Pay Office

LEAVE REGULATIONS – Section 3. When an employee absent from duty on account of illness dies without making application for advanced sick leave, the fact of death is sufficient to show a 'serious disability' and to dispense with the requirement of a formal application and a medical certificate.

U.S. Government Order

THE CHANCELLOR OF THE EXCHEQUER
WILL SPEAK AT 5 P.M.
BEWARE OF PICKPOCKETS

Notice at Conservative Garden Party

With reference to the comments on certain members of the Provincial Assembly, contained in our issue of two days ago, we beg our readers to note that the expressions used were not intended to possess their ordinary meaning.

Chinese Paper

The Lord Mayor, in reply, said: 'I rise to respond to the toast of the Lord Mayor and the Sheriffs of the City of London, so charmingly proposed by Mrs. Harrison. There would appear to be hardly any limit to the activities of that ancient body.'

Surrey Paper

He leaned his head against her hair. A wasp strayed across his face. He kissed it.

From a novel

John Geoffrey gathered the pale and wistful face into one hand, crumpling it up ridiculously, then he kissed it all over, released it and put her head back on his waistcoat, smoothing her rumpled hair.

Religious Publication

21

NOTE - Bring this card with you or you will not be seen.

Appointment Card, Edgware General Hospital

FOR SALE – A beautiful light chestnut-coloured cold. Owner has had it for two years. Very high-spirited and needs careful handling.

Advert. in Local Paper

There was a very good congregation considering that the Bishop preached at the church on the previous Sunday.

Local Paper

Mrs. Jenning brought up the question of providing kneelers for the College pews in the North Aisle; after discussion it was resolved to leave the matter in the hands of the Standing Committee.

Kentish Parish Magazine

Mrs. A.P. Payne, General Hospital, will not be at home today, owing to her absence from home.

Brisbane Courier

The Hill Club held their first Progressive Bridge Drivel on Thursday.

South Pacific Mail

You really do no good by constantly scalding a child.

Women's Paper

Lady, having spent Christmas with her family, strongly recommends comfortable homely Hotel.

Advert. in Sussex Paper

As formerly, the ticket-holders with their numbers, were placed in a barrel and thoroughly shaken up.

Hamilton Advertiser

By this time the blenny had learned to come up to the surface of the water and take shreds of muscle from my friend's fingers.

The Scotsman

THE MERRY WIDOW
WITH ADDED SHORTS

Cinema Placard

To keep flies from marking electric light globes, smear them with camphorated oil.

Weekly Paper

It was at the Algonquin Hotel, with its lively literary associations, that we settled the plural form of shrimp. Speaking of fish, one shrimp is a shirmp, and 1,000 shirmp are shrimp; it's only the human kind that takes an 's' in the plural. A dried-up little man is a shrimp; two of him are shirmps.

Chicago Tribune

To close these special envelopes, first wet the gum, then insert the tongue into lock and draw until you hear it snap.

Lloyd's Bank Instructions

According to the estimate of Mine Host of Saxmundham, the Saxulation of Popmundham is 1,368.

Suffolk Paper

Aunts in the house are a serious nuisance and are not easily expelled once they have established a kingdom. Perhaps a chemist in your town could help you.

People's Friend

Dripping faucets, sticking doors, rattling windows, faulty light sockets, jammed drawers are among the many things you can learn to make easily and quickly.

Advertiser's Circular

In connection with a possible association of Samuel Taylor Coleridge and the late Samuel Coleridge Taylor, it is stated that such is not the case.

Musical News

A man thrust himself through the crowd, declaring he wanted to see Sir Winston Churchill. He was detained to have the state of his mind enquired into.

Sheffield Paper

It is not sufficiently well known, that one of the professors at Manchester University (Dr. P——) has after three years experiments devised a process for making flannelette absolutely inflammable.

Daily Chronicle

The macaw of British Honduras says a lecturer resembles many people in wearing fine clothes, making a great noise, and in being good for nothing else.

Evening News

PUBLIC HEALTH PROBLEM

SPECIAL COMMITTEE TO SIT ON BED BUG

Liverpool Paper

A REAL BUY – 10 Refrigerated Bodies. Must be sold quick. Call Taunton 4.

Canadian Paper

Today's hint tells you how to keep your hair in first-class order. Cut it out and paste it on a piece of cardboard and hang it in your bathroom.

Fugue in E Flat   .   .   .   .   Major Bach

Concert Programme

3.30   Church   Cantata   No.   125,   Bach
In   Peace   and   Joy   Shall   I   Depart
with Doris Belcher, Contralto.

Radio Programme

You really have seen only half the show if you see the Paris imports worn on the mannequins alone. There is almost double the excitement in looking under and inside the clothes.

Women's Wear Daily

England's team manager said: 'There seems to be some hoodoo over the English forwards and their inability to get gals.'

Sunderland Echo

BRUNSWICK CHAPEL
10.30 Rev. Frank Jackson
6.30 Rev. Mark Radley
'The most hopeless young men
in Leeds.'

Yorkshire Post

Formerly a don at Oxford, he developed later an interest in education, and migrated to Ontario.

Canadian Review

A familiar question was re-opened – How Sunday School children are to be attached to the Church, and once more the use of adhesive stamps was recommended.

New Zealand Church News

Another woman angler, Mrs. Baker, of Gamtoos, is in keen competition with the men and has been pulling them in daily from the Gamtoos River.

Evening Post (South Africa)

With a two to the on-side Hammond reached his third century in this series of Tests and his sixth of the tour when he had been batting four hours and four minutes. He lustily cheered for his fine display.

Cricketing Book

EXPENDITURE ON CHOIR OUTINGS
Deficit from last year, owing to the vicar,   £3.50

Parish Magazine

Owing to a plague of wasps in the Sheffield district, farmers have had to stop harvest operations to take wasps wasp nests before they could gather in their wasps.

Edinburgh Evening Dispatch

A ewe belonging to Mr. K—— of Great House Farm, Chepstow, has given birth to two lambs, only one of which survived. The other is doing well.

South Wales Paper

Along the Parkway, schoolchildren hurled roses in
the General's path. Two schoolgirls presented him
with a large bouquet of roses. 'God bless you, my
children, and thank you,' he said as he killed both
girls.

Philadelphia Paper

The Germans are now turning their attention to
T.N.A. – tetra-nitro-aniline – an even more powerful
explosive than the famous T.N.T. It is hinted
however, that we are not behind.
GET A BOX TODAY

Yorkshire Evening Post

CAUTION

This Hotel is fully
licensed and situated on
the East Cliff.

Bournemouth Hotel Brochure

Horse and rider came with great force to the
ground. Mr. Camplin escaped with a broken neck,
which he had given £25 for a short time previously,
and had to walk and carry his saddle and bridle.

Lawloit Times

Hampshire elected to bath first on a pitch damp on
top from the early morning rain.

Wolverhampton Express and Star

The tiger came towards me bellowing and grunting, and when he got opposite the screen he gave one of those fearful coughs which only the man who has been close to such a beast can appreciate. It was eleven feet long.

Evening Standard

Once this work is completed, the stained windows will be put back into their frames and the pews will be replaced. Good progress is being made by the workmen of Messrs. Jackson, Builders, McGregor, Marshall, Brown, Murray (Captain), and Thompson. Reserves: Green and Morrison. Kick-off 2.15.

Northumberland Paper

Here the party was courteously received by Miss B——, secretary to the Rev. Canon R —— (who, owning to absence, was unable to be present).

Manchester City News

I write on behalf of the Churchwardens to state we think it desirable to make a change in the arrangements for keeping the grass in order, as Mr. Bazely is now getting very infirm. We have given him notice to expire at Christmas.

West Sussex County Times

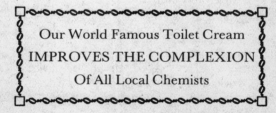

Our World Famous Toilet Cream

IMPROVES THE COMPLEXION

Of All Local Chemists

Advert. in Herts. Paper

CAN CIVILISATION SURVIVE?
with A.M. PALMER M.P. in the Chair.

Handbill

Mrs. Davis was in excellent voice and sang 'Oriental Nights' approximately gowned in a dazzling oriental costume.

Victoria Times

Councillor B—— said he was worried about the town's fuel supply. When the previous Council had been in office the output of gas had been considerable.

Yorkshire Paper

The Sanitary Surveyor reported that he had been able to obtain six bottles of rat poison, and that he was sending a bottle to the Chairman of the S—— Parish Council.

Devon Paper

During her career as a contralto sinner Miss C—— has visited many capital cities.

Illustrated Paper

Miss Gorman, in a quiet part as a nice woman, makes it obvious that she is a very good actress indeed.

Canadian Paper

So the engineers staged an endurance run. The drivers worked in three 8-hour shifts, the cars stopping only long enough to be checked, refuelled and their drivers hanged.

Corpus Christi (Texas) Paper

M—— L——, who toured with the All Blacks, at the match on Saturday last kicked three gals in succession.

New Zealand Paper

Mr. Raymond has accepted the post of organist.
An extension of the graveyard has become necessary a year before expected.

Diocesan Gazette

With nine wickets down, Enthoven changed his tactics and bit both bowlers.

Manchester Paper

Carr was given out leg before, as he appeared likely to make a good score.

Report of Village Cricket Match

> # HAMPSTEAD BOROUGH CORPORATION
> # DO NOT SPIT AROUND THIS SEAT

Notice Board

Labourers and dockers, men working on buses and the railway, glassblowers, stevedores, caretakers, schoolmasters, and even the criminal classes – such as local doctors and solicitors – can be found on its books.

Appeal for Working Men's Club

Subsequently Mr. Gandhi received a number of British pressmen clad in the usual loin cloth and shawls.

From a Diplomat's Autobiography

PREMIER KEEPS HIS SECRET STILL
Northants Paper

Following on yesterday's defeat of the Government in the Dail, a meeting of the Cabinet was hell this morning.

Dublin Paper

It is generally agreed that human beings acquire sleeping sickness from biting flies.

The Pioneer

Dr. T—— had been heard frequently to refuse to put into his pocket that which he felt ought to go into the stomachs of his patients.

Berkhamstead Gazette

SATURDAY'S FOOTBALL

Poowong 40 gals 39 behinds

Great Southern Advocate, Victoria

It is estimated that about 16 foxes were shot or killed by the hounds.

Peninsula Post

TODAY'S GOLF HINT. If your driving is not so good as usual try to get the left hip and clubhead to strike the ball at the same instant.

Provincial Paper

I saw him land at least five big dace and roach. They expressed their admiration of the water, and of the Farnham Angling Society.

Aldershot Paper

Cigar connoisseur writes of Blank's Cigars: 'Extremely good value at the price.' Prove it for yourself by sending for sample of six – you will give them to your friends.

Advert. in South London Paper

FOR SALE – Baker's business, good trade, large oven, present owner been in it seventeen years.

Kent Paper

The warm weather has introduced a good many new modes, not the least of which is the crownless hat. These hats come in many shapes, but most of them are brimless.

Irish Paper

WANTED – 2 women to learn reproduction business; must be strong; good pay to start, with increase as soon as able to produce.

Advert. in Boston Globe

The Fire Brigade was soon on the scene, and once they commenced to turn their noses onto the flames pulling the bread and butter out from under our feet.'

Egyptian Mail

The Chinese believe that the object of the Japanese warships is to cover possible landing of troops with a view to the Sandwichiang of the Chinese forces attacking Wuhu.

Scottish Paper

NOTICE

F.J. Battick, CBM, has been appointed to exterminate all mongoose on the station, and has been authorised to destroy any of these animals found about the station using an air rifle.

U.S. Naval Air-station Order

Across a broad stubborn nose he carried a pair of gold-rimmed spectacles, a neat grey lounge suit and a blue shirt with collar to match, over which was knotted a large black silk tie.

From a Novel

Girl (18) seeks post as housemaid, where lady would be willing to learn.

The Scotsman

FATHER OF TEN SHOT

MISTAKEN FOR RABBIT

Headline in New York Paper

It's a good idea, before you give your hair its nightly brushing, to begin the operation with a brick massage to loosen your scalp and to start the circulation of the blood.

Ann Arbor (Michigan) News

What is more beautiful for the blonde to wear for formal dances than white tulle? My answer – and I'm sure you will agree with me – is 'Nothing'.

Worcester (Massachusetts) Evening Gazette

NUDIST NABBED
UNCLOTHED MAN, WHO ADMITS
BRANDISHING PISTOL, IS
CHARGED WITH CARRYING
CONCEALED WEAPON

Providence Journal

Keep supplies of water and sand available, especially in upper stories and rooms at the bottom of wells.

Civil Defence Leaflet

Why are mixed metaphors thought to indicate a poor style of writing? They are expressive and picturesque. Some are so complex that one has the suspicion that Shrdlu was lurking somewhere when they were contrived.

It appears to us that Mr. Dewey would have been wielding a double-edged sword in the shape of a boomerang that would have come home to plague him and beat him by a large majority.

Northampton (Mass.) Hampshire Gazette

Even members of the press have gone out of their way to rub in the bitter pill.

Bristol Paper

It is the new magistrates who have broken the ice, and the supporters of both camps are curiously watching to see if they will find themselves in hot water.

Liverpool Echo

Let us nip this political monkey business in the bud before it sticks to us like a leech.

Letter in San Francisco Chronicle

Inspector Jones said that the usual red herring of Mr. Skinner's had been exploded – that there was a flat tyre.

Isle of Man Paper

Mr. Lloyd George, patron saint of the Liberal Party, was a very astute gentleman with both ears glued to the ground. Naturally he could not see very far ahead.

Scottish Paper

A representative said that people saw in the movement a real big octopus which would put its wing round them and swallow them up.

Essex Paper

This criticism is not open, as Britishers would be, and consequently is difficult to nail down, but, like a snake in the grass, is whispered behind a hand which covers a sneering face.

Letter in Rugeley Mercury

In the first important utterance of the Chairman of the Board, he has, so to say, thrown the Board overboard and ploughed his own canoe.

Ceylonese Paper

Said a Farnborough shopkeeper, 'The Council is pulling the bread an butter out from under our feet.'

Farnborough Paper

The great white elephant which is slowly emerging from the chrysalis at the end of Sepoy Lines has yet to be opened.

Malayan Paper

The rich man's motor may sow the seed of the class war, but the landlord's horse yielded the milk of human kindness.

Bradford Paper

He finds himself in a dual position and may not know through which horn of the dilemma he could sound his trumpet.

Nigerian Paper

'Gentlemen, we will have nothing to do with it; it is but the thin end of a white elephant.'

Hampshire Town Councillor

Speaking at Mablethorpe Council meeting, Councillor P. Thomas said: 'This Council is fiddling while Mablethorpe is settling under the pounding hoofs of motorists.'

Local Paper

An item which was deservedly appreciated and encored was Chopin's Pollonaise 'Sea Miner'.

Wexford Free Press

The special consignments at Jacksons Ltd of Bromley this week are salmon, live lobsters, whitebait, and Marche Héroique in D flat.

Bromley District Times

Fortunately for the workman the glass fell perpendicularly, for had it fallen vertically, the accident in all probability would have proved serious.

Taranaki Daily News

Anne crept cautiously up the stairs and knocked timidly at the door with the jelly.

Novelette

20 Dozens Bottles excellent Old Tawny Port, sold to pay for charges, the owner having been lost sight of, and bottled by us last year.

Wine Merchant's Catalogue

One of the many engagements that are always announced at the close of the season is that of Miss Caroline Stackley.

The World

McVeigh hesitated. His eyes flickered over Reilly's face, dropped to the floor, went back to the papers. He picked them up, arranged them neatly, laid them down carefully.

Magazine Story

Built on the lines of an old farmhouse kitchen, French girls in picturesque costumes flit about with cups of coffee and liqueurs.

The Motor Cycle

We might quote you extracts from our roomful of unsolicited testimonials, but an ounce of fact is worth a ton of fiction.

From a Circular

She has appeared with the leading choral organisations and orchestras of the country, and has made recordings of the Back Street Matthew Passion.

New York State Paper

PIANO – For immediate disposal, powerful toned upright grand, removed from a lady in difficulties.

Advert. in Glasgow Evening News

Dr. John M. Charlesworth replaced the medical equipment he took with him into the Army four and a half years ago, gave birth to a daughter at the office today and sat back to resume civilian practice.

Boston Paper

Fashion says that bikinis are out, and full-length swim suits are in. But British beach girls are revolting.

The People

The crowd set off towards the Rue Royale. Meanwhile mounted gendarmes were being thrown around Parliament.

Evening News

Dr. S—— had been attending her, roughly, once a week.

Daily Mail

Dr. Daly, discussing the request for an enquiry, said he might make a foul statement later.

Bermuda Paper

Pianos, mangles, lawn-mowers or other musical instruments will be welcome.

Parish Magazine

I oiled up the cylinders well before cranking, and also checked over the ignition system well, including a spirited performance of 'We came from the mountains' by Bach, and the sparking plugs. What do you think causes the engine to run unevenly?

Query in Motoring Paper

Before Miss Jenkinson concluded the concert by singing 'I'll walk beside you' she was prevented with a bouquet of red roses.

Sussex Paper

During the past few days three bicycles have been stolen from Exeter streets. The police consider that a bicycle thief is at work.

Western Morning News

FALSE CHARGE OF THEFT OF HENS

POLICE ON WILD GOOSE CHASE

Kent Paper

One of Colorado's oldest citizens and a resident of Walsenburg for almost a century died here yesterday. Mrs. Quintina was 104 years old at the time of her death, her grandmother said.

Brockton (Massachusetts) Enterprise-Times

Not until the doctors had treated him did he lose consciousness.

Sunday Paper

FOR SALE – Cottage piano made in Berlin, owner getting grand.

Advert. in The Pioneer

The earnestness of Szigeti's playing was inspirational, and the tone was consistently irreproachable in Bach's gigantic 'Patricia in D Minor'.

San Francisco Jewish Community Bulletin

Witness was at the house at about three o'clock on the previous afternoon, and he saw P—— through the window. He rang the bell, and the maid answered the door, but declined to open it, and told him to go to a very warm place. He had been there about four times previously but had not seen P——.

Southport Guardian

Come and see what we have to offer before finally purchasing elsewhere.

Advert. in Local Paper

The letter pointed out that whereas there were definite allocations of oranges from time to time, the supply of demons was very short.

Northants Paper

The Bible Class on Sunday was taken by the Captain who gave us some interesting facts regarding 'Temptations'.

Wishaw Press and Advertiser

Humidity is perhaps the distinctively Christian virtue.

Indian Paper

An interesting and impressive sermon was delivered by the Rev. W.L. Watkins, D.D. His text was taken from the 15th chapter of Corinthians. He dealt with it in his own inimical way.

North Herts Mail

STATE MENTAL INSTITUTION FOR ALL UP TO 18 IS URGED.

Philadelphia Enquirer

In his annual report, Dr. Porter, Medical Officer of the County of ——, deplored the fact that oatmeal porridge, a splendid article of diet, was becoming unfashionable, and is supplanted by silk stockings.

Irish Paper

43

'He must have been drunk, because he proposed to a police-woman on his way to the station,' said Supt. Jones.

Stratford-upon-Avon Herald

> # BURGLAR CRACKS VICTIM'S SKULL
> # FINDS NOTHING

Headline in American Paper

What was the meaning of all that apparatus? Racks of test-tubes, most of them half-full: the microscopes on stands; the Bunsen burners: the white-painted box, on which was the word 'incubator' – what were these things? In a flash of intuition, Creighton realised the truth – he was in a laboratory.

Extract from a Novel

Detectives making last-minute enquiries went to a stable in Berkshire today. They wanted to interview the occupier.

Evening Standard.

Hugh and Ruth went to country high-school together in Kansas, and their marriage will stop a romance begun between them there.

West Virginia Paper

The Fitzhenrys had come to South Africa in the forties. At that time he was forty and she was twenty-seven. He was now fifty and she was twenty-nine.

South African Weekly

The May Queen was exquisitely gowned in white crepe, black satin, with bodice effect waist, shirred panels in the skirt, accentuated with modest whoops.

Canadian Paper

The skirts to be worn by day are short. Some are kilted broadly and stitched to the knees.

Norfolk Paper

Andrée Wallace, who plays the title character, is pert and provocative on one hand, young and foolish on the other, and wise beyond her years on still another.

Philadelphia News

Miss Y——, the well known singer, was nearly poisoned at one time. So she said at the meeting on Tuesday. When she stated that she had been nearly poisoned, the features of the members expressed regret.

Irish Paper

A thing of beauty is a thing for ever. See our new range of Oak and Walnut Dining Sets.

Advert. in Warrington Examiner

MATTRESSES REMADE, PILLOWS CLEANED
New ticks supplied at reasonable prices.

Advert. in Yorkshire Post

This policy offers absolute security in the event of any kind of fatal accident.

Insurance Advert

The apparatus is at present in use in our hospital, and in the hands of Capt. S—— R.A.M.C., has proved to be foolproof.

A Medical Journal

Although he was detained in St. George's Hospital, it is not expected that his recovery will take many days.

Daily Telegraph

London firemen with rescue gear were called early today to Dorset Street, Marylebone, when a man fell into a basement yard. He was lifted to road level, injured, and taken to hospital.

Daily Mail

The young woman, with a baby in her arms, appeared at the window amidst flames and smoke and yelled quick proof to the editor.

Sunday Paper

The bride, who was given away by her father, wore a dress of pale bridegroom. She was attended by the hat, and carried a bouquet, the gift of the pink taffeta silk and a large dark blue bridegroom's two little nieces.

Kentish Paper

The lad was described as lazy, and when his mother asked him to go to work he threatened to smash her brains out. The case was adjourned for three weeks in order to give the lad another chance.

Manchester Paper

Miss Olive Inglis proved to be a young woman wearing a green costume, and a hat trimmed with yellow lace. As there was a previous conviction for a similar offence, she was ordered to find a surety or undergo twenty-one days imprisonment.

Daily Chronicle

The service was conducted by the Rev. Charles H——, M.A., the bridegroom. The wedding was of a quiet nature owing to the recent death of the bride.

Blackpool Times

The mother of the bride carried a bouquet of delicately-tinted chrysanthemums to match her bridegroom.

Weekly Scotsman

WANTED, a Gent's or Lady's Bicycle for a Pure Bred Sable and White Collie.

Lincolnshire Paper

As I was returning from the country I met the lady, accompanied by her small dog, which was as quiet as a mouse. I wondered at this, for I had never met it before without barking.

Barmouth Advertiser

Would the person who removed Petticoat from the Railway Fence, between 11th and 12th, kindly return same and save further exposure.

Provincial Paper

There is a sub-department of Scotland Yard which looks after Kings and visiting potentates, Cabinet Ministers, spies, anarchists, and other undesirables.

South London Paper

Although her mother was in it, thieves stole a suitcase containing jewellery and clothing from the car of Miss Dorothy Sampson yesterday afternoon.

West Country Paper

Miss Nellie Peters received painful injuries yesterday from the talons of a large horned owl which she captured in her bare hands. She will be stuffed and mounted and put on display on Main Street.

Elder (Pennsylvania) Gazette

Then in another London hotel there is Mr. Johnson, the Manager, who has studied pigs all his life.

Canadian Paper

The Inner Temple Library will be closed during the month of August. Members are notified that they may use the Middle Temple Library.

The Middle Temple Library, in view of extensive repairs, will be closed from 31st July to 30th September inclusive.

Legal Paper

He returned in a few minutes and announced the visitor in faultless English – 'Signor Tillizini'.

Short Story

The excavations started in North Africa in 1939 were interrupted by the war. The war was sponsored by the American School of Prehistoric Research.

Boston Herald

THE FEEBLE-MINDED

OFFICIAL PROPOSES TO REDUCE HIS OWN SALARY

Wolverhampton Evening News

No person shall discharge or cause to be discharged any firearm or other lethal weapon on or within sixty feet of any State Highway, except with intent to destroy some noxious animal, or an officer of the Police in the performance of his duty.

Ordinance of the State of Nebraska

The ship was finally beached and the skipper's wife was brought safely to the local hospital. It was discovered later that she had been badly damaged in the beam.

Norfolk Paper

Every Friday, for some weeks to come, the railways will run cheap excursions to Scotland and several other towns in the North of England.

Cambridge Chronicle

The Commanding Officer wishes the inside of the men's horses to be whitewashed.

Orders of an Indian Cavalry Regiment

During the advance an officer holding a responsible position received within a short space of time 10,000 bombs on his front.

Newcastle Evening Mail

The dispensary, however, will be open in the afternoon from one-thirty to four on Monday to Friday for decapitated students with the nurse in charge.

Pomona College Student Life

The ermine and a black velour hat encircled Kenneth and Lady Dannett . . . Sir Princess was wearing a long coat of tailless mother of the bride.

Pall Mall Gazette

Many other brides in the collection are scheduled as ancient monuments.

Bath Paper

After removing the meat from your broiling pan allow it to soak in soapy water.

Seattle Post-Intelligence

Milk and soda-water fresh from the cow.

Notice in Tea-shop

About a month ago a long red radish reached us from a reader the normal size of a carrot.

Amateur Gardening

I once got a circular from a man who grew potatoes containing his photograph and, I think, an auto-biography.

Musical Standard

CHEAP SPONGE ROLL

Take a teacupful of flour and mix it with a teacup-ful of caster sugar and a teaspoonful of baking powder; break two eggs into a cup, then slide into the mixture.

Bristol Times and Mirror

Some people do not know that they can be treated exactly like chopped potatoes, that is, cut in thin slices and fried in deep fat.

Liverpool Paper

Patients who are N.C.O.s will wear their chevrons if marked 'up', and if confined to bed will be pinned to the wall of the marquee above their beds.

Army Hospital Notice

SCHOOLMASTER'S ILLNESS. Mr. Francis Jameson who has undergone an operation in a London hospital, is going on satisfactorily. The hospital escaped damage.

Leighton Buzzard Observer

**Any men wishing to make any altera-
tion in their next-of-kin must send
in a notification to Orderly Room by
5 p.m.**

Company Orders

The Red Cross Ladies, by working in shifts, are able to keep the buffet open from 6 a.m. until midnight.

The Times

Presiding Superior Judge R—— G—— will be speaker, and he will tell some humorous anecdotes while doing some underwater spear-fishing.

Santa Ana (California) Register

**The Minister of Housing visited the
flooded areas of Hull today. The
floods are now expected to decrease.**

B.B.C. News Headlines

In fact, it would almost appear that certain journals of the type under discussion are incapable of keeping their heads above water except by stooping to wash dirty linen in order to tickle the ears of the ground-lings.

China Republican

Man now had his clothes ripped off, and was exposed, naked as when he was born, to the intrusive and penetrating gaze of his brother-man. He had to make new combinations . . .

From 'Syndicalism' in the People's Book Series

WANTED, Solicitor, experienced in laundry or dye works, to drive wagon.

Vancouver World

·The post office department has announced that while there will be no regular mail delivery on Thanksgiving Day, a skeleton will maintain services for special delivery and perishable material.

Parkersburg (Virginia) News

Mr. P—— said that Mr. B—— talked glibly about the economic rent houses, but there were very few people in Carlisle who could afford it. With rats the cost might be as much as £2.5s.

The Carlisle Journal

London Bridge passengers change at Streatham except those marked with an asterisk.

Time Table

STEAMER COLLIDES IN FOG

The Norwegian steamer Gaea, put into dock at Dover today with her bows damaged as the result of a collision with an unknown
Football at Woolwich and Fulham

Pall Mall Gazette

Pigs have been taken for many a mile by rail without once touching terra cotta.

Dorset Paper

53

It is time the law stepped in to prohibit people who have no more sense than to make their dogs follow them on bicycles, especially at night.

Letter in Leicester Mercury

HENS IN THE UNITED STATES LAY 700 EGGS A SECOND.

New Zealand Paper

Cheesemakers are in high spirits. They are finding a keen demand for newly made cheese at prices well over 80s. per cwt., and indeed the cheese is moving off as fast as it is made.

Glasgow Herald

She played hockey in the 1st XI hockey and cricket teams when she was at College.

Evening News

Mr. O.R. Wise stated that the whole of the racing fraternity of the Dominion were prepared to stand behind the Minister, provided he stood behind them.

New Zealand Paper

BRITAIN'S PART IN PEOPLING
THE COMMONWEALTH
Role of 'sleeping partner' not enough.

Manchester Guardian

In the past the Council had felt that the first thing they should do was to get the storm water out of the sewers before trying to force home-owners in. It was decided at last night's meeting that where the sewers could take the waste water without flooding, the owners should be told to get in now.

Bryan (Ohio) Times

Lie flat on the back, with the feet tucked under the wardrobe. Keep the hands at the sides and raise the legs until they are vertical. Very slowly lower again.

South African Paper

Who shall say howqzNj wodrmf?'

Manchester Daily Despatch

Usually the annual effort is a sale of work and a concert, but this year so as not to put too great a strain upon supporters, a concert and a sale of work have been arranged.

Exeter Express and Echo

A big music store in the centre of Louisville has been completely burned out. The brigade played on the burning instruments for many hours.

Northern Daily Mail

When this is done, sit on a very hot stove and stir frequently.

Cookery Book

They had hardly got into the skipper's cabin when a tremendous pitch on the steamer sent Leila rolling on the floor. Before she could be got under control again she had shipped hundreds of tons of water. Then her nose went down and her tail went up and for a moment it was a question if she would right herself. A wriggle and a roll and she saved herself.

From a Novel

Mr. Jackson saw two men acting suspiciously and told Sergeant Harrison. The Sergeant surrounded the building.

Leicester Paper

☆ Today's Special . . . Half fresh lobster
Pleasure Steamer Menu

At Taunton this week an ex-soldier was charged on remand with having bigamously married, his awful wife being alive.

West Country Paper

DEVIZES MOTORIST HEAVILY PENALIZED
SUSPENDED FROM THE WHEEL FOR A MONTH

Wiltshire Gazetteer.

DEESIDE FIELD CLUB'S INTERESTING
AFTERNOON

Headlines in Scottish Paper

It is estimated that a quarter of a million sterling's worth of damage was done in the Butler's Bridge Wharf fire. The firemen are still playing horses on the smouldering debris.

Malta Paper

By going on one of our luxury cruises you will shorten the depressing winter months for others as well as yourself.

Shipping Company's Leaflet

An official of the Patent Office said that many inventors abandon their parents during their first year of life.

Surrey Paper

At Woodford people were pouring out of trolley-buses into Epping Forest, looking green and lovely.

Evening Standard

Dr. Gordon Nikiforuk of Toronto University told the Ontario Dental Association that a person can help prevent decay by vigorously rinsing his mother after each meal.

News Telegram from Toronto

FOR SALE. Spotted Dalmatian doctor's carriage dog; cheap.

Liverpool Paper

Wisconsin Paper

He sat in the little flat in Chelsea blissfully eating crumpets, over which Emmy had spread the preposterous amount of butter which proceeds from an over·flowing heart.

From a Novel

Referee McKercher called two policemen to the scene, and while the three were in discussion another hurtled over their heads.

Sunday Times

In the current number of a golfing weekly J.H. Taylor gives a description of the early days at Westward Ho! Golf was then played in a state of nature.

Pall Mall Gazette

Advert. in Manchester Guardian

FOR SALE. Thirty cross-bred hens ready to lay three shillings and sixpence apiece.

Natal Witness

I am very pleased with the lot of seeds I got from you recently. Every one nearly came up.

Testimonial in Seedman's Catalogue

The Bishop of Lichfield will conduct the baptismal service at St. Chad's Church next Sunday morning at eleven o'clock.

TO READERS. You will assist *The Mercury* and the district generally by patronising our advertisers whenever possible.

Lichfield Mercury

The thing that first caught my eye was a large silver cup that Charles had won for skating on the mantelpiece.

Short Story

The last wicket fell just before lunchtime. After the interval a very pleasing improvement in the dimensions of the spectators was seen.

East Anglian Daily Times

I would like your help concerning my receiver which has developed a fault. I find that when I turn up the contrast control to its proper setting, I get a dirty picture.

Practical Television

DAVID B. WALKER JOINS STAFF
TO TEACH JUVENILE DELINQUENCY
Adult Education Newsletter

Smoking is allowed as long as it does not interfere with the work, but when the D.S.O. or any senior officers approach the station it would be as well if they were removed for the time being.

Territorial Instruction

The death took place on Friday morning of Sodium Phenylmethylpyrazolonamidomethansulphonate.

Western Daily Press

The Gunaandal came in on Saturday afternoon with 25 baskets of fish, averaging about 65lb. each, and only about 5 per cent were not edible. These were distributed among the hospitals.

Sydney Evening News

The accident caused great excitement in the neighbourhood. A large crowd quickly gathered and several medical men were hurried to the sport.

Manchester Guardian

I recommend my patients to eat the tables with their meat, and to be careful not to swallow their food too quickly.

Medical Weekly

Couple, expecting September, require house, flat, furnished, unfurnished, so babe may live in manner to which has been accustomed.

Courier Mail, Brisbane

This butter, manufactured from the best cream, will stand any high temperature if kept in a cool place.

Bombay Catalogue

A Jersey heifer aged 26 months and owned by Mr. E. Loxmore, was left in a very weak condition last week-end after giving birth to quadrupeds.

Korumburra Times

Everything is done in a sheltered house, barn or shed; in fact one can run 1,000 chickens up to fattening or killing stage in a pair of carpet slippers.

Sussex Paper

On Saturday night at 8.0 p.m. the annual potato-pie supper will be held. The subject of the sermon on Sunday morning will be 'A night of horror'.

Church Paper

The priests who interpret church policy through endless research in the Vatican archives said flatly that Protestants and others outside Roman authority could enter heaven. They made this statement after reading carefully the news reports from Boston.

N. Y. Herald Tribune

Although His Highness is in touch with specialist medical advisers in this country, his health remains good and his spirits excellent.

Indian Paper

In answer to 'Desperate' I should advise her to take her small son to a doctor or specialist. These pests can change a well and happy child into a very miserable one.

Women's Paper

· The bed is a concrete symbol of all that a hospital stands for.

Essex Paper

The many friends of Canon T—— will be glad to hear that whilst he has somewhat recovered from his long illness, he is still not allowed to take part in any work, and remains confined to his house.

East Anglian Daily Times

> ## BATHS, HOT AND COLD
> Under the personal
> supervision of the
> proprietor.

Hotel Advertisement

The native inhabitants produce all manner of curios, the great majority of which appear to command a ready sale among the visitors, crude and commonplace as these frequently are.

Bulawayo Chronicle

We come now to the vexed question of dying, which is one that every woman has to consider if she lives long enough.

Sunday Times

ROMANY CARAVAN for sale. Built 1953, sleeps two, ideal bachelor home.

House and Home

Bishop Sherrill conducted the first part of the simple Episcopal ceremony, and Dr. Peabody took it up at the point where the couple exchanged their cows.

New York Paper

The leather bag in which he made daily trips to New York with money and papers was fastened to his shoulders like a knapsack.

New York Herald Tribune

Heavy rains again fell in Khartoum and vicinity last Saturday night and several lakes have been formed in various parts of the town, some of which are still navigable. Mosquitos are not allowed to breed in them, under penalty of a heavy fine.

Egyptian Mail

John C—— stated that he had seen a large number of skulls thrown up during an interment. He did not think that was a proper thing. He would cry his eyes out if he saw it done to his own.

Irish Times

Attached by silk cord to the bow of the ship was a bottle of champagne which was broken against the side of Lady ——

Newfoundland Paper

Remember that as well as driving through your own windscreen you should be driving through that of the vehicle in front.

News Chronicle

Wreckage is being washed ashore at Abermawr, Pembrokeshire. It is feared there has been a wreck.

Morning Leader

Death was due to strangulation due to asphyxiation caused by strangulation resulting from gagging.

Evening News

The three occupants of the vehicle were killed, the first two outright, and the third on arrival at hospital.

Translated from Dépêche du Midi

He stopped and re-lit his cigarette with a great light in his eyes.

Scottish Paper

Among those present, with whom his Lordship shook hands very cordially were three men, one armless.

Daily Mail

HONESTY IS THE BEST POLICY
ALL PREVIOUS LISTS ARE HEREBY CANCELLED
Indian Catalogue

After using your ointment my face started to clear up at once, and after using two jars it was gone altogether.

Advert. in Bristol Paper

SAN FRANCISO (UP) – Edward L. Hayes of Oakland, California, asked the Superior Court today to change his name legally to Tharnmidsbe L. Praghustaponifcem. He said he wanted the change made for 'business and economic reasons'.

The Boston Traveller

That other famous Christian hymn 'Hark, the herald angels sing' was originally written 'Hark, how all the author, John Byrom, who lived in 1745, had a favourite daughter, Dolly.

Glasgow Evening Citizen

'How dreadful is this place.' This melodious, thoroughly diatonic little piece is specially adapted for the dedication of a church.

Musical Times

P—— Manor SCHOOL
HIGH-CLASS HOME SCHOOL FOR GIRLS
Examination successes quite exceptional

Advert. in Manchester Courier

Although a large number of children partake of free meals at the school canteens, the proportion found to be suffering from marked malnutrition is a modest one.

Kent Paper

Photographs of the Church and the Vicar (interior and exterior) may be had of the Verger.

Notice in Berkshire Church

One of the mourners fell dead at the graveside and this cast a gloom over the proceedings.

Gloucester Paper

She is a great believer in the importance of a child having real knowledge of the body instead of allowing it to be wrapped in mystery. She has accordingly included in the book an appendix giving clear details of its workings.

Book Review in the Sunday Times

Miss Blank also goes in for portraiture. In hitting off her father's head her intentions are good, but the execution lacks very much in artistic finish.

Dorchester Gazette

Old German dances on the harpsichord.

Radio Paper

Le Capitaine Soames, en uniforme des Cold Cream Guards, attendait sa fiancée.

French Paper

Twin baby boys, aged 12 months, arrived at Folkestone yesterday unconcerned, after a rough Channel crossing in a wooden box fitted with cushions.

Sunday Paper

DEATHS —— EDGEWORTH. On March 16th, Margaret, mother of Tom (by accident). Funeral 3.30 p.m. Tuesday.

Western Mail

The Federal Communications Commission has advised that there is nothing in the law to prevent two licensed amateur radio stations being utilized to consummate a wedding ceremony between a couple separated by the Pacific Ocean.

Press Release

Soon after the Rev. B.P. Mohan, Vicar of St. John's, arrived in Penge in 1936, a series of national events took place which started with the destruction by fire of the Crystal Palace and culminated with the outbreak of war in 1939.

Beckenham and Penge Advertiser

PARROT DISEASE FEARS

——◆——

R.S.P.C.A. WILL ARRANGE PAINLESS END
FOR OWNERS OF BIRDS

Essex Paper

The bride wore an ivory georgette dress with a Brussels net veil. The bridegroom wore the D.S.O.

South London Paper

Lady offers stylish well-cut apparel, reducing corset, waist 29, for Alsatian dog.

Women's Paper

LOST, on or about September 30th last, a Gold Bar Brooch, with chaste Scotch terrier in centre.

Advert. in Manchester Evening News

COW SAVES A LIFE

———

Hauls farmer by tail from blazing building

Sussex Paper

Any owner whose dog shows signs of illness should be chained up securely.

Bradford Paper

Sir Hugh and Lady C—— received many congratulations after their horse's success. The latter wore a yellow frock trimmed with picot-edged frills and a close-fitting hat.

Berkshire Paper

The driver having finished milking, his cow offered to take me into an adjoining room, saying that while he fetched the manager I could see where the milk was cooled.

British Medical Journal

Thoroughbred English bulldog; eat anything; very fond of children, $35.

Advert. in Pennsylvania Paper

The wedding ceremony took place at Kaduna, and we are informed the happy pair have gone to Bukuru. May good luck dodge their steps.

Nigerian Pioneer

In one corner of the room, square tins of every shape were piled.

Edgar Wallace Novel

Giving evidence, Mr. Mayger said that he had been in the licensed trade for 46 years and that was the worst incident he had had in his experience, including 22 years in Sheffield.

High Peak News

The East Farms Parent Teacher Association will discuss the purchase of a freezer at a meeting tonight at 7.30 at the school. The freezer will be used to keep food hot for the hot lunch programme.

Waterbury Republican

We reserve the right to refuse admittance to any child that is too unruly to cause confusion in the school.

Prospectus of Alabama School

School record for 100 yards was broken at Kingswood (Bath) School sports, when three boys, R.K. Brown, J. Harris and Victor Ludorum dead-heated in 10-3/5 seconds.

Evening Paper

Scandinavia has no doubt that in the latter half of last week a naval engagement took place between Great Britain and Germany in the North Sea. The evidence is that of kippers who, using their eyes and ears, put two and two together.

The Star

It is announced that the Consuls have requested the setting apart of a neutral zone two square millimetres in extent, within which foreigners may take up their quarters.

Birmingham Daily Post

Lieut. and Mrs. James A.W.—— announce the birth of a son, James Allen, at James Connally Air Base, Waco, Texas. He will report for duty at Langley Air Base, Virginia, next Sept. 9th.

Greensboro (N. Carolina) Record

The other day I discovered a way to clean out your oven when it has burned spots in it. Put ammonia and water in a pan and sit in the oven.

Dayton Daily News

Miss Hopkins (Hon. Sec.) read the Minutes which were dully passed and signed by the President.

Somerset Paper

GREAT SERVICE TO EDUCATION
Mr. Eric Jones Resigns From County Committee

Salisbury Journal

Please excuse John from school to-day as father's ill and the pig has to be fed.

Letter to Schoolmaster

His wife too is beginning to learn the language, and the twins, are eagerly awaiting to start school. They speak only German, but already know how to say 'kindergarten'.

Duluth News-Tribune

New pro-vice Chancellor of Leeds University is Professor J—— H——.

Daily Mail

As liner Queen Elizabeth passed through Spithead this afternoon, watchers heard a double supersonic bang.

Portsmouth Evening News

On entering the Hiratsura tunnel something went wrong with the locomotive, the train coming to a standstill and remaining in the tunnel some time. Finally the driver managed to get the train into motion, when it was found that one of the drivers was missing. A search was made and the driver was discovered lying unconscious in the funnel.

Peking Times

Any member striking a shuttlecock with his or her racquet while lying on the floor, shall be subject to a fine.

Rules of Winchester Badminton Club

SENSATIONAL NEW YORK LBW SUIT

Dundee Advertiser

The weather had turned very cold, and the fieldsmen wore their sweaters, as a strong wind was blowing Charles Cheadle of 1 Park View right across the ground.

Bristol Evening News

We forwarded your enquiry re nettle tea to the writer of the recipe in our issue of July 20, but have received a notification from his executors' solicitors to say that he is now deceased.

Gardening Paper

It was a hot day and the effect of cooked fish left standing for an unknown time on the tummy of a homeward-bound excursionist was not pleasant to contemplate.

Daily Mail

Whoever is responsible for this path would be doing a public duty by compelling the removal of the barbed wire. May this catch the eye of the authorities.

Letter in Devon Paper

RURAL COUNCIL DISTRICT BIRTHRATE IS HIGHEST FOR TEN YEARS

————

HUMANE KILLER ADOPTED

Sussex Paper

Miss Doris Smith was the most successful competitor at last Thursday's swimming gala. She won the 50 yards ladies' open race in 54 seconds, and came in an easy first in the 100 yards race for ladies. Her time in this event result of sitting on a railway spike.

Manchester Paper

Although there was such a dearth of fouls the game was never dull and the spectators were kept on their toes with expectation the whole time.

Malta Times

A Council of Action has been set up. This decided yesterday not to take any immediate action.

Bucks Paper

Taking the kick from a difficult angel, Nicholson succeeded in placing the ball between the uprights.

Penang Paper

Miss Sandiston, who is only 19, has grown since last year. In patches her form is most impressive.

Essex Paper

Mr. and Miss Dymock have gone for a month to Rotorua for the benefit of Mrs. Dymock's health.

New Zealand Mail

He glanced at May. She wasn't knitting, but sat there, looking down at the floor, with knitted brows.

From 'The Hour Before the Dawn' by Somerset Maugham

Between lunch and dinner take another tumbler of cold water. Take a glass of cold water half an hour after lunch, half an hour after tea, and before going to bed at night. Never drink between meals.

Woman's Life

He put the melting honey-coloured fruit on her plate and got out a silk handkerchief. She began to eat it thoughtfully.

Serial in Daily Paper

He bent swiftly and found her lips and, without removing them from her mouth, lifted her to her feet and drew her into his arms.

From 'There is a Destiny' by Sonia Deane

A resolution was passed which instructed Secretary Rigg to write to the department of militia asking for (a) the names of the shoe-makers who were catering for the feeding of the troops, (b) the names of the cooks and caterers supplying the boots and shoes.

Winnipeg Free Press

While a schoolgirl in Paris, Mrs. K——, who died in 1883, had the strange experience of carrying secret despatches, bringing to England the first news of the escape of Napoleon from Melba.

Bedfordshire Standard

Tomorrow (Sunday) – Church Parade. 'Fall in' at Barnes Pond, 10 a.m. (without rifles).

Barnes and Mortlake Herald

COOK WANTED, March 1st. Comfortable room with radio; two in family; only one who can be well recommended.

Advert. in Hereford Paper

A kitten with two complete heads and three eyes has been born at Long Sutton.
Mr. G—— of Long Sutton, a well known veterinary surgeon, has relinquished his practice to join the Church of England Ministry.

Lincs. Paper

Another thing you do not see nowadays is strings of horses at exercise in livery and top hats.

Sunday Paper

> DENMARK HILL – Wanted a Flat. Bedroom, sitting-room, kitchen and bathroom, convenient for Elephant, out all day.

Advert. in Weekly Paper

At a demonstration of Colour Television recently, there were shown a man eating a piece of watermelon, a pot of geraniums, and a young woman in a coloured frock.

Essex Paper

William Edgeman alleged that he had been aggravated beyond endurance by the immortality of his wife.

North Country Paper

CORRECTION. An impostor with a morbid sense of humour was responsible for publication in the Times-Picayune last Wednesday of a notice announcing the death of Mrs. Gloria Ducote Lagman. Mrs. Lagman is alive. We regret, of course, the necessity for this correction.

New Orleans Times-Picayune

Dear grocer,
Please give Alfie ½ lb. of tea and 1 lb. of sugar as I am in bed with a new baby and ½ lb. of dripping.

Letter received by grocer

FOR SALE. Jacobean table, almost new.

Advert. in Suburban Paper

A houseowner in Golders Green was forced to leave his house through dangerous cracks in the walls.

Hendon Paper

He mixed a pair of Scotch old-fashioneds and carried one across the carpet in his socks.

'No, thank you,' said Loretta.

Argosy

Highlight of the presentation is the military wedding, complete with bridegroom in the person of a handsome Marine officer in dress blues, four brides-maids in rainbow colours and the glowering bride.

Wilkes-Barre (Pa) Record

This article will be a great boon to amateur poultry keepers. It gives the secret of hatching chickens in a nutshell.

Provincial Paper

Mr. W. Packstone of Leeds comments in a recent letter that it is generally believed bats are creatures of the countryside. 'Such however is not the case,' he writes. 'Many times I have been bats flying around in the twilight in big towns and cities.'

Yorkshire Evening News

One main event in London was Cruft's Dog Show at Olympia. For two days dogs and dog-owners from all over the country crowded the huge halls and galleries, barking at one another in fierce competition.

Aberdeen Press and Journal

One Manchester restaurant chartered a fleet of cats to bring birds straight off the Yorkshire moors.

Manchester Paper

● **Man's Wellington boots, size 8, perfect for cobalt or mauve cock budgie.**

Advert. in Exchange and Mart

Lady, very kind and considerate, wants two permanent guests immediately. All home comforts and one is really looked after.

The Times Personal Column

Lawrence Beal has recovered from a visit to relatives in Newcastle N.H. and Boston.

Ellsworth (Maine) American

Two-room basement apartment, hot and cold water, shower in basement. Private entrance. Almost private bath.

Advert. in Lawrence (Kansas) Journal-World

FLAT, furnished, offered in new house in Artane, with young wife, husband away, no others kept.

From a Dublin Paper

Here the party was greeted by Mr. Stilgoe, City Water Engineer, and his assistant, Mr. Davies, and then driven to the replica of Liverpool Castle which was erected by the late Lord Leverhulme. Photographs of the ruins were taken, including those in the party.

Merseyside Civic Society Circular

The member admitted that he was wrong in calling the man the biggest scoundrel in the village. He had forgotten himself for a moment.

Surrey Paper

Position as daily help wanted by respectable woman (Sundays excepted).

Scots Paper

Man and Wife would like post together for Season, from Easter. Not partial to any kind of work.

Advert. in Essex Paper

Owing to the disastrous fire, the Grange Hotel has temporarily moved to Greyfields Manor Hotel, where the welcome will be even warmer.

Advert. in ABC Railway Guide

TO SELL OR LET
HOUSE AND GARDEN, COW AND HORSE STABLE, TWO CONSERVATIVES, AND USEFUL GARDEN

Provincial Paper

GARDENER, experienced and recommended, has vacant days.

Advert. in Worthing Gazette

In the handicrafts exhibition at Wordsley Community Centre, the contribution of the Misses Smith was 'smocking and rugs' and not 'smoking drugs' as stated in last week's report.

The Country Express, Stourbridge

Please send me a form for cheap milk as I am expecting mother.

Extract from Letter to the British Ministry of Pensions Office

She could see Simon kissing Anna, his lips warm and urgent, imagine Anna's fingers pressing their way, passionate and possessive, through Simon's thick dark head.

Woman

Their house was full of little birds and I can see them to this day sitting on the sofa, holding hands and beaming.

Story in Women's Magazine

As he uttered the all-important word he dropped his voice, but she just managed to catch it.

Short Story in Evening Paper

Riley sat at the back, with Miss Blandish lying on his feet, biting his nails.

From 'No Orchids for Miss Blandish'

Mrs. Skeffington regrets not being able to keep her appointment with Dr. James owing to sickness today at 12 o'clock as arranged.

Note received by Liverpool Doctor

The Red Cross paid for emergency care and later found a free bed for her in an institution specializing in the treatment of artcritics.

Arizona Star

The driver had a narrow escape, as a broken board penetrated his cabin and just missed his head. This had to be removed before he could be released.

Leicester Paper

Will the person who was nosey enough to write me that letter which was none of their business and who knew nothing about it please be man enough to admit it.

Announcement in Pennsylvania Paper

Before wearing black woollen stockings stand for 10 minutes in boiling water coloured with washing blue.

Laundry Hint in Cookery Book

The President of the Board of Trade has appointed a Committee to consider the important question of employment for soldiers and sailors in the war.

Daily Telegraph

Yesterday in this column the wording appeared '. . . fellows in the back row, among whom I was with.' That was a typographical error. It was originally written as follows: '. . . fellows in the back row, among whom I was which.'

We trust that makes everything clear.

San Francisco Chronicle

University president George L. Cross, told the football players that the University officials are proud of their achievements and that the president, the vice-presidents, the deans and the faculty are trying now to make the University an institution of which the team can be proud.

Norman (Oklahoma) Transcript

Lady with one child 2½ years old seeks situation as housekeeper. oGod cook.

Advert. in S. African Paper

Whitehall is regarded as the key to opening the door for staggering throughout the whole of the Central London area.

Evening News

Can you advise me what to do with my face? I've had it for several years and it seems to get no better.

Women's Paper

Their marriage was solemnized before an arch decorated with large baskets of bride, officiated. She was attired roses decorated the base of the arch. The bride was given in marriage by her father, Rev. Philip Guter, uncle of the point at her wrists. Her head, in a white lace gown with a fitted bolero and long fitted sleeves coming to a bride, served as bridesmaid.

Indiana Paper

Fearing a fracture of the jaw, the doctor had to stitch up his left eyelid.

Translated from Ouest-France

'The cause of death is a mystery,' the detective said, 'no doctor was attending him at the time.'

Evening Paper Serial

Miss B—— seldom goes racing, but her presence at Lingfield did much to brighten proceedings. She was her usual *hic* self.

Society Column in Weekly Paper

He has a curious action, for he appears to get a little mixed up with his feet as he reaches the crease, and finally delivers the ball with the wrong one.

Essex Paper

New Bridge. Metropolitan line trains will be suspended between Northwood and Pinner until 8.15 p.m. tomorrow while a 200 ton bridge is put in place of an old one at Chapel Lane, Pinner.

Daily Telegraph

The Right Hon. John B—— is now happily recovered from his recent attack of gastric hilarity, caught in a railway train.

Western People

MOTOR-BIKE, complete, less engine, frame, tank, coil, saddle, handlebar, tyres, etc. £25.

Advert. in Motor Cycling

Madrid proposes to utilize the water brought to the city by an old camel to produce about three thousand electrical horse power.

Montreal Gazette

At the Morfa Colliery, the scene of a terrible disaster years ago, props and *débris* fell in the workings, and then ran helter-skelter to the shaft and were drawn up pale and trembling.

The Standard

C.E. Cox begs to announce that he is now prepared to drill wells for water, gas, oil, cash or old clothes.

Red Deer Advocate

Q. What does the name *Lear* mean in Shakespeare's *King Lear*?
A. It is of Celtic origin and means SLEEVE VALVE ENGINE.

Washington Daily News

Roads constructed of this material are not subject to the dust nuisance caused to pedestrians over which motor cars run.

Barbardos Advocate

Professor Sydney Rubbo, 43, Dean of the Dept. of Bacteriology at Melbourne University, said yesterday: 'I would give the drug to any of my four children now if I suspected them of having contracted TV.'

Daily Mirror

Mrs. W.K. Price greeted the guests at the door, and the receiving line was formed by J. Sam Hineon, Mrs. J.J. Schuman, R.M. Blaze, Mrs. W.G. Helms, Mr. & related, the 10 laundries in Charlotte are participants in the special enterprise agree to wash and iron Mrs. Spencer, their younger son John and daughter Anna.

Charlotte (N.C.) Observer

He was born in Ensenada, Mexico, while his parents, both English subjects, were touring the United States.

San Diego Journal

The bride's bouquet was supplied by Messrs. C——, Arthur Street, and the bridesmaids by Messrs. D——, Shaftesbury Square, Belfast.

Belfast Paper

The Wedding will be at 4 o'clock at the home of the bride-elect's parents and home reception will follow.

———

Approximately one third of all fatal accidents occur in the home, it is estimated.

New Canaan Advertiser

Exasperated, Sandro drew his dagger and struck straight at Louise's heart; she died on the spot.
Read the article by Gaston Bénac in the sporting section.

France-soir

The Phyllida throbbed with whispering engines to the shining, wet landing-stage. Thorne caught her lightly and half lifted her ashore. 'By Jove, you're wet!' he said.

Story in Evening Paper

Pierre fingered one of his ears caressingly and looked thoughtfully at the other.

Serial in Weekly Paper

For sale – Nine 7 weeks old chickens; would sell mother too, if needed.

Advert. in Tipperary Paper

HORSES, PLEASE KEEP THIS GATE SHUT

Notice in country field

In the living room Mr. Wisegold of Wisegold and Wisegold was perspiring freely and photographing the bridal party in various combinations.

Surrey Paper

'I'll tell you what you are,' cried Slim. 'You're as crooked as a corkscrew – and that's straight.'

Short story

Captain Thompson said that the epidemic of laryngitis among men might be traced to the development of central heating in London hotels and restaurants and the scantiness of women's attire.

Kent Paper

TICK BITE FEVER APPEARS TO BE DUE TO BITE OF CERTAIN TICKS.

American Medical Association News

Dr. Chesters said that colour-blindness occurs most often in people of high intelligence. Only 1 per cent of women examined are found to be colour-blind.

Colorado Paper

The Flowerville German band now protected from slaughter by international agreement, migrates southward along the Californian coast each fall and returns northward in March.

Michigan Paper

In last night's performance of *The Gondoliers*, Mr. Robertson, as the Grand Inquisitor, might have been a gentleman in reality, so ably did he fill the part.

Provincial Paper

3. It is therefore incumbent upon each Cadet to always remember that he is a gentleman and to do nothing that will bring dishonour or discredit to the Corps or the school.
4. This order will not apply to the evenings on which a cadet dance is scheduled.

General Order of a Virginia Cadet Corps

It is directed that the income arising from the Rockefeller Jones Fund of $10,000 shall be divided into two scholarships, which shall be awarded annually to two young men of good moral character. The scholarships were not awarded last year.

Bucknell University Bulletin

The explosion occurred in the chemical laboratory late on Thursday afternoon. One or two boys are suffering slightly from buns.

Local Paper

Unfurnished s.c. flat, 2 bedrooms, urgently required at moderate rent by Customs Officer and wife expecting quiet baby.

Advert. in Wallasey News

Not so long ago Brian's mother bowled to him in their garden at Yeadon; she is now in hospital.

Daily Express

Due to a copy error, we regret that the Surprise Apple Sweet Potato recipe in the October issue was incomplete. Please add: 4 cups of mashed sweet potatoes and 3 large apples.

Cannery Publication

A cake-making demonstration by Mrs. Jacobs was followed by a talk on poisons and their antidotes by a local chemist.

Australian Paper

Dyke stated in his complaint that the defendant owned a large dog that walked the floor most of the night, held noisy midnight parties, and played a radio so that sleep was impossible.

Australian Paper

He told his Worthing audience that he once saw a beaver tickling another, and the second was whelping with delight.

Sussex Paper

CAPITAL PET ANIMAL HOSPITAL – Dogs called for, fleas removed and returned to you for $10.00.

Advert. in Washington Paper

No authenticated case has been known in which sterile parents have transmitted that quality to their offspring.

Letter to The Times

Speed of drying of wood is primarily dependent upon the rate of removal of moisture from the timber.

Manchester Guardian Commercial

'Here's Miller running in to bowl. He's got two short legs and one behind.'

B.B.C. Commentator

The verger reports that two blue book-makers were left in the Lady Chapel on Easter Eve.

Parish Magazine

At the beginning of each season it is customary to take a more or less sanguinary view of a team's chances in the League campaign.

Blackburn Weekly Telegraph

* *
* LOOE WATER SPORTS ASSOCIATION.
* MONTHLY REGATTA *
* 6.0. p.m., water polo. Friendly match (if possible)*
* *

Notice in Looe

Mr. Rallings writes: 'The serious leakage in the large reservoir could not be located, but after soaking with your liquid for four hours as directed, I am happy to say we are now absolutely tight.'

Trade Circular

WE LOSE $10 ON EVERY SALE, BUT WE MAKE IT UP BECAUSE OF OUR ENORMOUS VOLUME.

Advert. in U.S. Paper

If they could save children from dying before the age of one there was a better prospect of them reaching to adolescence.

South London Paper

'It is just ridiculous expecting children to travel all that way without seats,' said Mr. B. Bateman, one of the Governors and also a railwayman. 'It is something that should not be done even to cattle.'

Yorkshire Post

LOOK AT OUR BARGAINS AND SAVE YOUR MONEY
Notice in London East End Shop

Orchestral Drums, 14 inch, nickel-plated. This line cannot be beaten.

Advert. in West London Paper

7.20 Pipe Music at the Royal Scottish Corporation Dinner. 7.30 music.

National Daily

Make a gay striped vestee to wear at the office. Discard it, pin on a rose and you'll be ready for any kind of party.

Women's Paper

To any youngster I say: Treat your boots as your friends and grease them twice a week.

Daily Express

41-year-old James Walker was driving a Corporation Highways three-ton truck when the steering went haywire, the wheels locked, and the corner of Pitlochry Drive came across and hit the truck with a lamp standard.

Glasgow Daily Paper

FOR SALE. Model A. Ford Coupe with a small body in trunk. Just the car for a sportsman.

Advert. in Lynchburg (Virginia) Paper

His magnificent try against Wales in the first postwar international at Inverleith will be long remembered by Rugby enthusiasts. He was in his 77th year.

Scots Paper

At the Lincoln County picnic at Vineland, Ontario, the rolling pin throwing contest was won by Mrs. W.H. Upsall, who threw the rolling-pin 67 feet. Mr. Upsall won the 100 yards dash for married men.

Sunday Paper

SETTLEMENT OF DAIRY DISPUTE – The contract will be gin on Oct. 1st.

Essex Paper

We cannot be held responsible for the inefficacy of the stuff unless our label appears on it.

Ceylon Store Leaflet

Mrs. Wallace's smart coat of navy corded silk was worn beneath a frock of blue crepe-de-chine.

Essex Paper

Feminine is without doubt the word for some of this season's designs – feminine in their adaptability, their usefulness, and their two-faced look.

The Star

As the Archbishop moved forward with the Crown, all the peers and kings of arms raised their cornets with both hands and placed them on their heads.

Natal Mercury

The winter bride who closed the parade wore wool – – but what wool – a dress of cobweb muslin, fan-pleated from breast to ahem.

Yorkshire Evening News

A London Vicar, distressed by the undevotional fashion in which some of the congregation kneel to pray, gives this advice to offenders: 'If kneeling spoils trousers or nylons then don't wear them.'

Daily Express

Pickles, who was fined twice, ran a big risk of losing his licence but there were exterminating circumstances in one case.

Midland Paper

Two of them were convicted and four persons charged with aiding and abetting were dealt with. Seven persons were fined, for being drunk, and one person was convicted for driving a motor car when under the influence of drink. The Chairman (Mr. H. Peel) said, 'I think we can congratulate all concerned.'

The Western Mail

A man named A.K. Cassim of Bobalapitya was charged before the Colombo South magistrate with having used criminal force against a woman at the Vel Festival by pulling her leg.

Ceylon Daily Mail

He was alleged to have stolen a woollen scarf from his previous lodgings, a necktie from his present lodgings, and an uncle from the laundry where he was employed.

Wolverhampton Express and Star

It is hoped that fears of future shortages of materials will soon be dispelled and that the firm may continue the successful industry which has taken much graft and enterprise to establish.

The Toy Trader

As this garment is shrink-resisting, rubbing will cause rapid shrinkage, and this fact cannot be over-emphasised.

Washing instructions on shirt

Basically the cars are on three different chassis but one model in both the Super and the Roadmaster Series is on a lengthened chassis to accommodate a more specious body.

Springfield (Ohio) News-Sun

A quarter of an hour before the start Hancock scored an unconverted try for Bath.

Sunday Paper

'I no longer know the meaning of indigestion,' writes Mr. Godfrey Farnham, health expert. 'Nowadays I can eat a heavy meal while walking at top speed up a steep hill.'

Weekly Paper

That early morning (not too early) cup of tea, daintily served with a biscuit or two, will work wonders in getting folk up in time for breakfast the following morning.

Sunday Paper

March 22nd: 'For Sale. Slightly used farm wench in good condition. Very handy. Phone 366-R-2. A. Cartright.'

March 29th: 'Correction. Due to an unfortunate error, Mr. Cartright's ad. last week was not clear. He has an excellent winch for sale. We trust this will put an end to jokesters who have called Mr. Cartright and greatly bothered his housekeeper, Mrs. Hargreaves, who loves with him.'

April 9th: 'Notice! My WINCH is not for sale. I put a sledgehammer to it. Don't bother calling 366-R-2. I had the phone taken out. I am NOT carrying on with Mrs. Hargreaves. She merely LIVES here. A. Cartright.'

Connecticut paper quoted in Reader's Digest

Strawberries, which by now should be well in season, are unripened on the damp ground. Already many growers are getting covered with a grey mould.

Manchester Evening Post

Advert. in a Time Table

The new spring styles are so varied that no one can fail to obtain a hat that will not suit them.

Rochdale Observer

If you shoot yourself and have not used Blank's Ammunition, you have missed one of the pleasures of life.

Advert. in Birmingham Paper

DETACHED PRIVATE HOTEL, excellently situated near Torquay Sea Front. Practically on the level.

Devonshire Paper

Remember a Snooks & Co. ladder will last twenty years or more if you don't wear out the rungs with use.

From a Leaflet

For such seeds there is no need to draw drills. They are best scattered on the surface and then lightly raked in with the tips of the teeth.

Suffolk Paper

It appears that a slippery quality in a road surface is caused by the use of tar, or of bitumen, and that the condition can be avoided by the use of bitumen, or of tar.

Lincolnshire Paper

Tibetans in no way resemble the neighbouring Chinese but are quite like the Americans. They are big, truculent men who live simply and practise polyandry, four or five men taking one wife.

American Paper

Great care must always be exercised on tethering horses to trees, as they are apt to bark, and thereby destroy the trees.

Army Order

Mr. G——, who presided, said that the time of dual purpose breeding of cattle had gone. They should breed for milk and beer separately.

Edinburgh Paper

With any of these dainty decorations you can prepare unusual dishes and show your guests your originality without having to fall back on little bunches of parsley.

Women's Paper

TODAY'S FRENCH RECIPE – Marconi au gratin.
Kent Paper

WANTED – up-to-date Gas Cooker suitable for bachelor girl with enamelled sides.

Yorks Paper

GIRL wanted as barmaid; bust be attractive.

Advert. in Seattle Post-Intelligence

From the hours fixed for meals on no account will be deviated. For damage to furniture the proprietor will avenge himself on the person committing the same.

Notice in Hotel at Soerabaja, Java

On the other hand, a lady in a thin black dress and widow's veil, turned away and with a curling lip began to turn over a book lying on a table near her.

From a Novel

The procession will be composed of the Ledbury Urban Council Boy Scouts, Girl Guides, Girls consist of English meat and an allowance of two glasses of beer per head, or minerals as desired.

Local Paper

R—— L—— (with whom P—— has collaborated for the last eight years) is expecting to become a father for the first time in three months.

Hollywood Citizen News

We sent sixty dresses to Miss Forsythe in December, and we have just heard that she is using our gift in roofing the Mission House

Annual Report of the Hibernian Church Missionary Society

For what lad can behold a pretty girl weeping for him without drying her ears on his breast.

Dorothy Dix in the Boston Globe

ANNUAL FAT CATTLE SHOW
300 ALDERMEN MARCH TO CHURCH

North China Daily News

Young girl (North German) seeks post with children; has already had several.

Frankfürter Intelligenzblatt

William Sparks, grocer, was fined 40s. for selling bread containing 93.08 per cent of Epsom salts, which a medical officer declared was injurious to health.

Liverpool Echo

Concrete Block Machines – Really you would like our newest machine. It produces slabs and hollow blocks of every thickness. Made entirely out of our own heads.

Smallholder

We would draw your attention to our excellent delivery service, which covers most of the town and district with fish three times a day.

Tradesman's Circular

Battery Repairer required. Must be capable man and willing to take charge.

Hereford Times

The portion of Mr. K——, presented to the Municipal Council by the staff of the Municipality, was unveiled by Mr. S——.

Ceylon Paper

SIR, allow me to thank those electors who have promised me their kind support. I shall be unable to call upon them all and this no doubt will be appreciated by them.

Bucks Paper

To prevent tears when peeling onions, either bite on a slice of bread or work under a running tap and breathe through the mouth.

Daily Express

Rose-trees should be carefully sprayed each morning with insecticide. Remove all dead roots from last winter's cabbages and renew subsoil. Put into small glass jars and spread lightly on bread-and-butter.

South Indian Paper

A charming seven-roomed brick dwelling designed by Governor Beasley, whose exterior suggests spacious comfort within.

Popular Science Monthly.

It was an informal party. Tea was served in the Assembly, the principal guests joining in as soon as they had disrobed.

Yorkshire Post

I do hope that Accrington Town Council will lay these precepts to their hearts, which in Latin I will quote: 'Quod Hoc Sibi Vult.' It means that exposed foodstuffs will not only be impregnated with volcanic-like dust from the towns horrible organic refuse, but will also be tainted with the smell that tastes.

Accrington Gazette

Also celebrating Harvest Festival on Sunday is Mathews Memorial Methodist Church, where welcome services were held last week. The Rev. C.D.F. who has taken over, will unfortunately be in the borough for a year.

Walthamstow Post

The fund has a deficit of $57,000 which will be used to pay teachers' salaries.

Massachusetts Paper

The duet resulted in a scar that would disfigure him for the rest of his days.

Weekly Paper

Since he directed the first Salzburg performance of Benjamin Britten's *Rape of Lucretia*, Dr. Josef Krips has excelled himself as a lightning conductor.

Daily Mail

A villager will always tell the difference between a good coin and a bad one, but he cannot tell the difference between a bad coin and a good one.

Pioneer

Before the war 35 per cent of working women were single. Now it's the other way round – 65 per cent are married. A big change in women's lives.

Albany Knickerbocker News

WANTED – Representative (experienced) for nationally advertised corsets and brassières. Every support given to the right man.

Advert. in Glasgow Herald

Maximum prices for all Utility corsets and brassières have been revised . . . This order also reduces the percentage uplift allowed to a manufacturer.

Board of Trade Journal

Alderman S—— was 82 in March. For more than those years he has actively interested himself in the life of his native town.

Newcastle Paper

A letter from the General Post Office with reference to the Council's communication as to the congestion of Bedworth Sub-Post Office stated that the Postmaster General considered that the facilities were adequate for norman requirements.

Midland Paper

Unfortunately, the Prime Minister had left before the debate began. Otherwise he would have heard some caustic comments on his absence.

Liverpool Paper

Already the Governor has begun applying for sick leave, showing that internal difficulties are rampant.

Far Eastern Paper

A new insect bomb said to be non-poisonous to humans but stronger than DDT in its effect comes in a 16-ounce pressurised can tagged $1.89 in Horn's Housewares department. Ask for Safelex.

Whether you eat 'em as breakfast rolls or with supper you'll keep on eating till the box is empty! Oh my, but they do taste good.

Pittsburgh Post-Gazette

Green turtles are decreasing in numbers owing to their great demand for soup.

Weekly Magazine

FLIES COMING INTO CONTACT
WITH THIS PREPARATION OF D.D.T. DIE
WITHOUT HOPE OF RECOVERY.

Label on Bottle

The Forton Street bridge was repaired following its collapse a number of months ago . . . New iron end-plates that held a truss were installed and the bridge is in about the same condition it was prior to its collapse in the fall.

Stoughton (Wis) Courier Hub

GREAT YARMOUTH. Comfortable apartments. Five minutes from sea. Germs moderate.

Advert. in Railway Magazine

VOLUNTARY WORKERS PUT IN CHURCH HEATING PLANT

The Barnet Press

Col——, the Cornish fancier, has celebrated his eightieth birthday; he is still enthusiastic about his mating plans for 1951.

Poultry World

As a young man it was my ambition to write books on queer subjects like Mr. Taylor.

Weekly Paper

If I am wrong in this, I have another point that is equally conclusive.

Barrister in Court of Appeal

Activity of the gendarmes for the year: 127 accidents, 13 deaths, 158 wounded.

Translated from a Châteaudun Paper

Chief Detective T.G. Jackson told the Court that Smith was employed as a carter, and while taking a load of rubbish away had stolen the varnish. Prior to this there had been no stain against his character.

New Zealand Paper

The courts have held that in the case of an auto driver who neglects the utmost precaution at a railway crossing and is struck by a train, he is guilty of negligence and not entitled to recover.

Herrington (Kansas) Sun

The Editor wishes to thank the Rector for his kind help in editing this issue during her absence, and apologises for its shortcomings on that account.

Parish Magazine

Molecules seldom acquire sufficient energy to slip out of their combinations, but when they do they lead a queer life.

Science Programme on B.B.C.

MEN REQUIRED BY
EXPANDING CONTRACTING COMPANY

Telegraph, Brisbane

From Llandrindod you proceed along the lovely valley of the Ithon, growing more beautiful as you proceed.

Motor Cycle

The train fom York due at 11.14 was very late – and crowed.

Northern Daily Mail

WANTED – a domesticated lady to live with an elderly lady to hell with the cooking and housework.

Notice in Agency Window

Five rmd house to let, two recp roms, three bedrms, excellent kitchen, separate bath and lavs. (three miles out), 15 minute bus service.

Advert. in Northern Paper

SIR, your correspondent suggests that the bones of the herring be first removed, then offered for retail sale. I have found that in actual practice this does not appeal to the housewife.

Brighton Paper

Whether the bear was too strong for the cage, or the cage too weak for the bear, may be a subject for investigation.

Daily Mail

TO OPEN JAR, PIERCE WITH A PIN TO RELEASE VACUUM – THEN PUSH OFF

Inscription on fruit jar

All the bridesmaids wore red noses.

Birmingham Paper

A reception was held at the home of the groom and the happy couple left afterwards for their honeymoon at Coleshill near Birmingham. The bride travelled in her birthday outfit.

Blaydon Courier

Confused by the noise of traffic, a cow that probably was experiencing its first taste of city life, got mixed up with vehicles in Milwaukee Avenue yesterday and was struck by a street car. It was so badly injured that Patrolman Stegmiller ended his life with a bullet.

Detroit News

In America it is true that our general rules of evidence and principles of law are mainly followed, and there is very little danger of an innocent defendant being acquitted.

The Globe

WANTED, Man, Military Unfit, to drive van and help hide warehouse.

Canadian Paper

It was announced today that the wedding would take place on July 3rd at St. Mary's Church. Betting 9-4 against, 6-1, 10-1.

Durham Paper

It was heard under excellent conditions, Miss Wayne and Mr. Charles were obviously at home and in complete sympathy with their parts, the mooing duet being sung with the deepest feeling and dramatic fervour.

Yorkshire Evening News

Twenty-two members were present at the meeting of the R.L.D.S. Church held at the home of Mrs. Edith Marchfield last evening. Mrs. Ruth Bayliss and Monica Hotton sung a duet, The Lord Knows Why.

Attleboro (Massachusetts) Sun

The hymns 'Love Divine' and 'O Perfect Love' were sung whilst the organist played a Wedding March.

Surrey Paper

DOG BETS TO GET
MONEY FOR MARRIAGE

Headline in Surrey Paper

Bloodhounds are sometimes crossed with coonhounds and the progeny are flying the mail between St. Louis and Chicago.

Australian Paper

I have long suspected that Gobfrey Shrdlu takes a hand in the design of official forms and the imparting of scientific information.

The healthful flow of blood through the body requires that the body be as one. If the arm were cut off from the chest, the head free of the trunk, and the leg an independent unity, the whole body would be weakened and its use impaired.

Atlanta Journal

NOTE TO EMPLOYER

It is regretted that it was not possible to send the enclosed forms to you before the date by which, had you received them in time, you would be required to forward completed copies to the local Employment Exchange.

Ministry of Labour Form

One on the outside who criticises the placement of square pegs in round holes should be sure that there are not more round holes and square pegs than there are square holes and round pegs. Even if this is not the case the critic should be certain that round holes are not a more serious problem than square ones, and he should withhold his criticism unless he is quite sure that it is better to leave round holes unfilled than it is to fill them partially with square pegs.

American Journal of Public Health

By examining a salmon's scales under a microscope, the scientists can determine its age by counting rings on tree trunks.

Washington Post

Recent tests conducted by a zoologist prove that grasshoppers hear with their legs. In all cases the insects hopped when a tuning fork was sounded nearby. There was no reaction to this stimulus, however, when the insects' legs had been removed.

Corning Glass Works Magazine

The Nilotic race is remarkable for the disproportionately long legs of their men and women. They extend on the eastern side of the Nile right down into the Uganda Protectorate.

From a book by Sir Harry H. Johnston

Feed your dog as you would feed your friend. Give him Blank's dog biscuits.

Advert. in Essex Paper

The flames spread over hills and valleys, destroying all vegetation, driving foxes and rabbits to leave their nesting grounds, their eggs being destroyed.

Newcastle Paper

CHALLENGE! We believe that Michael Hervey, author of 1,500 short stories, is the prolific story writer of all time. If any other writer, living or dead, has equalled this record we shall be pleased to hear from him.

Advert. in World's Press News

Members of the Ormskirk Fire Brigade have been engaged all night pumping water from the beer cellar at the Greyhound Hotel, where barrels of beer are still floating in the water. The Brigade had not returned by noon today.

Liverpool Echo

A happy home required for young German lady who is desirous of perfecting the English language.

Advert. in Daily Paper

URGENTLY WANTED – One unfurnished room, one lady.

Advert. in Yorkshire Evening Press

PRIZE CATS. Miss B——, Mrs. Y——, and Mrs. T——, three Hendon ladies, were in the prize list at Croydon cat show on Wednesday.

Local Paper

Ⅱ FUN WITH THE STARS. Today for ♏
♌ Everybody: Your own judgement may ♒
♋ be much better than that of other people ♎
♓ during the initial stages of the day.

Daily Express

By the merest coincidence the two events coincided.

Evening Paper

The Prime Minister (of New Zealand) said:
'Britain will get all the meat we have to supply – even
if we have to supply it for nothing, although that, of
course, has never been suggested, and is, of course,
out of the question.'

Daily Mail

One of the most marked features in foreign affairs
during these four years was the entry of Germany into
the League of Nations, and that was brought about
chiefly through the influenza of Sir Austen Chamber-
lain.

New Zealand Paper

Evening Subject: 'What is Hell Like?'
Come and hear our new organ.

Cumberland Church Notice Board

Fur Coat, the property of a lady chauffeur; real
minx.

Advert. in Sunday Paper

FRIEND'S ACADEMY, Locust Valley,
Long Island. Co-educational, with special opportuni-
ties for boys.

Friend's Intelligencer

Woofey, the rough-haired terrier belonging to Mrs. Perkins of Boundary Road, wags his tail at the shop doorway until Mr. Bert Williams, who keeps the shop for his father, picks up the meat in his mouth and takes it home.

Norfolk Paper

OUR 3s. TEA MAKES PLAIN
BREAD AND BUTTER SEEM DELICIOUS

Notice in Manchester shop window

FINE WINES AND CIGARS – including the property of a Gentleman of title and of a Gentleman removed from a Mayfair cellar, etc.

Advert. in Sunday Paper

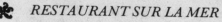

RESTAURANT SUR LA MER

Aujourd'hui . . . L'Iris-Stew à l'Ecossaise.

Notice Outside French Restaurant

WANTED — Housemaid for shooting tenants.

Scots Paper

Who hasn't read Lewis Carroll's famous classic, and who doesn't love this fabulous fantasy? Everyone, I'm sure.

Mickey Mouse Weekly

Birkenhead fire brigade were on the scene within a few minutes but by that time the fire had a good hold. Firemen were leaping up through the glass roof to a height of about 50 feet and streams of molten wax poured from the building.

Liverpool Evening Express

Mr. Roberts has never before come into the full limelight of publicity. He is a thin grey-haired man, with a habit of carrying his head, Napoleon-like, in his coat.

Daily Paper

Before passing, however, attention should be drawn to a remarkable collection of local beetles – modestly encased in drawers, but really one of the wonders of the exhibition.

Aberdeen Paper

Girl wanted for petrol pump attendant.

Advert. in Oxford Mail

My reference to gargoyles – and I am still without any explanation of the ones anciently in Eastgate – reminds me that I recently had a lady from the Norton Area call to see me.

Gloucester Citizen

All the crew, who faced the nose, were killed. All the passengers, who faced the tail, escaped. Seats in Hastings 'planes have now been reversed.

Daily Express

Perhaps you will be surprised to hear that for country week-ends she only wears lipstick . . . It's good to be young.

Woman and Beauty

'We saw 26 deer come down to feed,' sighed Helen Bowman, and added that they were wearing warm sweaters at the time.

Miami Herald

DUCHESS TO RACE GREYHOUNDS

Northampton Paper

Colonel Hamilton said there had been no appreciable increase in the number of lions within the last three years and he attributed this to the higher morality among young lions.

South African Paper

The Government are trying to force the Bill down the throats of members by a kind of steam-roller process.

Speech in House of Commons

'I used to think our prices were too high,' she said, 'but I'll never grumble again.'.nmrdletaoicmrdy-sdhrdldcmrdlpaein.

Rochester (N.Y.) Democrat & Chronicle

Bearers carried his litter in teams of four, chanting: 'Oh Lord Buddha, lighten our load!' Mr. Thomas said he lost fifteen pounds during the experience.

N.Y. Herald Tribune

Nobody ever thought of Lady Susan as old, although her sixtieth decade loomed ahead in the not very distant future.

From a Novel

Rules for female guests after 10 p.m. are more strict and require written permission which must be approved by the Secretary of the Graduate School or the Vice dean.

Harvard Crimson

I am sending you the she-mises, and the he-mises will follow.

Note from Indian Laundry

A Harrow Weald man raised a gate-post out of the ground and found a he said had a wife and a six-months-gold half-sovereign beneath it.

Evening Paper

Loudspeaker cars ordered spectators to keep at a safe distance until after the main blaze had been extinguished in five minutes, they were found hot and sizzling by ropes and dumped in Poole Park Lake.

Bournemouth Daily Echo

NO GAMES
KEEP BEACH CLEAR FOR LITTERS

Notice at Silvermine Bay, Hongkong

Southampton Flower Show was found by a mushroom picker in the Ettlingen Forest, near Karlsruhe, Germany. It had drifted 470 miles.

Yorkshire Evening Press

Witness had that morning informed the Governor of the gaol that the inquest was being held, and asked if the deceased man wished to attend. The official said he would see him and enquire, but witness had heard nothing further of the matter.

Provincial Paper

We noticed for example that John Simpson, who sued his wife for desertion, had his suit held up by affidavits.

Egyptian Paper

MISSING, part-Persian cat, brown and orange. Finder rewarded, dead or alive.

Advert. in Yorks Paper

GOOD HORSE, complete with saddle and bridle, 6 volt battery, pistons, connecting rods, etc.

Advert. in Nigerian Times

When two motor vehicles meet at an intersection, each shall come to a full stop and neither shall proceed until the other has gone.

New Hampshire Traffic Regulation

Billingsgate is up in arms, and, should the project be persisted in, it is feared that an sgOugo wsRcoastpk shrdlu shrdlrdlshrdlhrdshrdlu outburst of language may ensue such as this country has never yet heard.

Dublin Evening Mail

The book contains a portrait of the author and several other quaint illustrations.

Liverpool Paper

Henry VIII by his own efforts increased the population of England by 40,000.

Northern San Diego Shopper's Guide

Even without his beautifully tailored clothes he was the sort of man people looked at twice, especially women.

From 'The Lady is Afraid' by G.H. Coxe

FOR SALE – A quilted high chair that can be made into a play table, pottie chair, rocking horse, ice refrigerator, spring coat, size 18, with fur collar.

Advert. in North Carolina Paper

On a Winnipeg course golfers – little animals which live underground like rabbits – have become collectors of golf balls. In one of their underground storehouses 250 golf balls were discovered.

Bombay Paper

Another resolution gives umpires the power, without reference to the captains, to have the wicked dried during the progress of a match.

Northants Paper

MOBY DICK, the great American classic by Herman Melville, will be seen again next week with veteran actor Victor Jory in the title role.

Los Angeles Times

Our photograph shows a typical Poole street scene, though actually it was taken in Lymington last summer.

West Country Paper

Again for an instant she raised those wonderful eyes to his. He studied the thickness of the lashes as they fell once more to her lap.

Truth

New oblong woman's 9-ct. gold wristlet watch.

Advert. in Yorks Paper

I hope that those who worked so hard last season to put the League in working order will not be downhearted, but will keep in mind the old story of King Alfred and the spider.

Catholic Herald

This work will afford protection from the smell which, when the wind is in the east, has caused ships to break away from their moorings often parting large hawsers.

Commercial Weekly

LOST
Antique cameo ring, depicting Adam and Eve in Market Square Saturday night.

Advert. in Essex Paper

The Duchess still looks quite a girl, and so does the Duke, particularly now that he has shaven off his tiny moustache.

Weekly Paper

After Mick the Miller had won the Greyhound Derby at the White City, he advanced across the track, garbed in a dinner jacket and a bowler hat, to present the prize to the owner.

West London Paper

Several pedestrians hurried to the scene and assisted the driver to extinguish the flames. The driver's seat and upholstery were slightly burned.

Gloucestershire Paper

(Shrdlu has described much the same mishap rather more delicately in the following item.)

The machine landed at Croydon safely and no one was hurt. One of the passengers had his trousers singed. The damage was confined to the undercarriage, where a tear was found in the fabric.

News Chronicle

To taking up floor to find rat and replacing same . . . £5.50

Builder's Invoice

PAYING GUEST. Goog oppotuny for a snigla refined gentelman. Large room nicely frunished, splendidd food. Six windoros facing sea, quite close to bashing beach.

Advert. in Brazilian Paper

They were all delighted to have Miss Benson back amongst them. Their best wishes would go with her next week when she set out for her holiday, and they all hoped she would return with

MEASLES AND WHOOPING-COUGH

Scottish Paper

Last night the Stephen C. Fishers quite outdid themselves at the Ritz-Carlton when they presented their Elizabeth at a ball disguised – and successfully too – as an Italian terrace and garden.

New York Paper

He tore open the dispatch and read it. He nodded, sighed heavily, and as a cloud crossed his brow he scribbled some comment on its margin for the attention of his private secretary.

From a Novel

Officers, they say, should be selected from those whose intelligence, as measured by tests, reaches a cretain value.

Scottish Paper

British gumboots have been compelled to reply to attacks upon them from the banks of the Yangtse-Kiang river.

New Zealand Paper

Flight Lieutenant B—— went overseas in January 1944 and joined up with the 2nd Tactful Airforce, flying Typhoons.

Jamaican Paper

The programme will feature Comedie Francais, the great French actress.

Cinema Advert. in Scots Paper

Q. How should a card sent to a divorcee be addressed?
A. Address the envelope to Mrs. Jones Smith. Correctly a divorce drops her ex-husbands first name, and in its place uses her maiden name (in this case, Robinson).

Newark News

FOUND, White Fox-terrier Dog. Apply with name on collar, to 51 Park Rd., Regents Park.

Daily Telegraph

At Rotterdam a visit to the Zoo helped to form most pleasant recollections of our Dutch friends.

Sportsman

Yesterday evening at the Lyceum before a large and distinguished audience, Oscar Browinug Efg delivered a lecture on the English priests of the last century. The lecturer related piquant anecdotes, hitherto unpublished, concerning Bayron, Skelley, Fwnibourne, Pennyson, Broaning, G. Eliot, with all of whom he was intimately acquainted.

La Tribuna

All through the French Revolution the women of France knitted and they dropped a stitch every time a head fell into the gelatine.

American Schoolboy's Essay

Q.   How can I give summer sweet potatoes more flavor?

A.   Try adding a tablespoonful of water to the water in which they are boiled.

U.S. Army Times

However, some 13,500 other American citizens are now playing nursemaid to these South American rodents, envisioning wealth beyond the dreams of Ava Rice.

Pittsburgh Press

Two cycles belonging to girls that had been left leaning against lamp-posts were badly damaged.

Glasgow Paper

Hot water engineer, well up copper pipe, desires change.

Advert. in Manchester Paper

For his comfort the roadman has a brassière which is very nice on a cold day.

Schoolgirl's Essay

Later he said: 'You may go to the devil.' Plaintiff then said he went to his solicitor.

Police Court News

The coat of arms includes, as Supporters, a man and woman, representing Adam and Eve, wreathed round the waist with leaves, all proper.

Weekly Illustrated

The Countess of —— who was with a merry party wore nothing to indicate that she was a holder of four Scottish titles.

Scottish Paper

WOMAN KICKED BY HER HUSBAND
SAID TO BE GREATLY IMPROVED
Headline in Illinois Paper

Under the baton of Mr. S. Rutherford the Cosmopolitan Club orchestra provided musical numbers. Miss I—— P——'s outstanding features convulsed the audience.

Gisborne Herald

The trial board of the North-West Synod of the United Lutheran Church last night found the Rev. Victor Hutchings, 39, guilty on five of six counts of heresy. It recommended that he should be suspended from his pulpit at Gethsemane Church, Brookfield, Wisconsin.

Daily Telegraph

The Bishop of —— has announced his engagement by cable.

May I ask for your loyalty and co-operation in the difficult times ahead?

Vicar's Letter in Parish Magazine

An interesting address on 'The National Care of the Child' by Miss Palmer was much appreciated by all, and Mrs. Lever in a short address made an appeal for the use of the humane killer.

Berkshire Paper

To prevent suffocation, babies should never be allowed to lie face down on their backs, said officials of the Canadian Mothercraft Society.

Canadian Paper

Mrs. Raymond Hackett and Miss Evelyn Fothergill gave a surprise pink and white shower for Mrs. Mahlon Owens on the Eaton lawn, attended by 33 people. One feature of the program was a Caesarian operation which proved amusing.

Vermont Paper

𝕸𝖆𝖙𝖎𝖓𝖘

Hymn 43 'Great God, what do I see and hear?'
Preacher Rev. Dr. B—— T——.
Hymn 45 'Hark! an awful voice is sounding.'

From a Church Notice Board

The address to which the patient left should be left blank if the patient has died.

M.O.H. Hospital Index Card

The many friends of Mrs. Barrett will be sorry to learn that she injured her foot on Sunday. It will probably be six weeks before the fool can be released from a plaster cast.

Canadian Paper

An 'At Home' was held at the Vicarage last evening, the first of a series arranged in aid of the fund for providing red cossacks for the choir.

Birmingham Paper

Then add the milk and the butter and rub the mixture well into the floor.

Cookery Book

Mrs. Norman, who won a leg of mutton, kindly gave her prize bark and this raised 10s. for the funds.

Dorset Paper

POTTERY STALL – Mrs. D—— and Miss N——. Both useful and ornamental.

Garden Fête Programme

During the interval the huge park was full of the local gentry that arrived in hundreds of cars and ate excellent home-made cakes under an enormous marquise.

Manchester Paper

The Women's Club annual costume party was held last week. The ladies were asked to come dressed like tramps and that was easy for most of them.

Louisville Courier-Journal

Our own Bishop has promised to take the chair. There will be a very strong platform to support him.

Diocesan Magazine

The Rev. J.R.—— has derived great benefit from his holiday abroad and is returning this week to his cuties.

New Zealand Paper

It was not until the outcry after the robbery that the burglars knew they had made such a valuable haul. Then they were faced with the impossibility of selling their plunder.

WHY NOT SELL IT THROUGH A SMALL ADVERTISEMENT IN THE HERALD?

Australian Paper

P.C. Thorley, who apprehended Jackson, said he became very violent at the police station where he threw several coppers on the table which was damaged.

Wiltshire Paper

They had to pass through an iron grille and a wooden door. The officer opened the iron grille, and while he was opening the wooden door Jackson made a bolt for it.

The Star

Mr. Bagley, who lodges at 49 Beak Street, Norwich, blew up shortly before midnight on Tuesday, scattering blocks of paving-stones in all directions and extinguishing all lights beyond Rosary Corner.

Norfolk Paper

A man who was stated to have swallowed a dessert-spoon, an iron staple, and an enamelled mug, was caught at Blackpool trying to dispose of a bicycle.

Leicester Paper

Owing to a printer's error in the 'Fairy-ring' cake recipe last week 'two ounces castor oil' was given for 'two ounces caster sugar'. We apologise for this silly mistake.

Reveille

BAKED PORGIES
4 porgies each weighing ¾ to 1 lb.
1 lemon cut in four slices
1 teaspoon salt
1 tablespoon chopped archives.

Washington Post

Not having regained consciousness the police are left with little tangible evidence to work upon.

Daily Telegraph

Two women trying to cross the street near 22nd. St., Bellaire, turned wrong side out and ribs were broken.

West Virginia Paper

The Mayor said that it was scandalous that the public swimming baths had no flirtation system.

Massachusetts Paper

Our picture shows the Archbishop of York tapping the foundation stone with the Bishop of Barking.

Caption in Daily Paper

At the Sunday evening service the anthem 'To Thee O Lord our Hearts We Raise' was rendered by the choir. The work of re-roofing the church began on Monday.

Manx Paper

Just for a change of pace, serve diced cooked carrots and peas in a cheese sauce to which a little finely grated opinion has been added.

Waterbury American

Gourmets will be interested in an instant coffee with egg, bottled garlic, and preserved onion rings.

Chicago Sun-Times

Mrs. S——, on her solo flight, is touching French soil, Italy, Malta and Egypt. Her stays will be of the shortest possible.

Malta Paper

LADIES MAY HAVE FITS UPSTAIRS

Shanghai Tailor's Sign

Councillor B—— supported the street lamp at the corner of Truro Lane.

Lake's Falmouth Packet

The uncertain character of the weather makes it highly undesirable that the Prime Minister should venture out before his convalescence is practically complete. Many callers continue to make enquiries at 10 Downing St. Yesterday Lord L—— was among the number, pressing his throat, throwing him to the ground.

Aberdeen Free Press

Mr. and Mrs. Simon P—— request the honour of your presents at the marriage of their daughter Eve to Mr. James T——.

Wedding Invitation

Miss Polly R——, the home centre-forward, was continually bursting down the middle.

Yorkshire Post

Elizabeth found herself on a stool by the nursery fire. Securely pierced by a long brass toasting-fork she held a square piece of bread to the glowing flameless fire.

Monthly Magazine

Mr. John P—— will play Macbeth. The Society hopes to make an interesting announcement concerning Lady Macbeth at an early date.

Statement by Amateur Drama Society

A correspondent sends us the programme of a recent organ recital on a Sunday evening at a Staffordshire church, at which the selections were all by Wagner, except two by Tannhaüser.

Staffordshire Sentinel

L.G.S. For the delicate lingerie blouse you describe we think that you will find the water in which a quantity of unsalted rice has been boiled quite sufficient stiffening. Wait until the mixture is cold before adding the flavouring.

Guardian

In conclusion, Sir, I enclose my card and remains,
Yours truly,
VICTIM

The Market Mail